T0320690

# STRATEGIC A2/AD IN CYBERSPACE

*Strategic A2/AD in Cyberspace* focuses on exclusion from cyberspace, or the ability of a state to be cut off entirely from cyberspace. Strategic anti-access and area denial (A2/AD) operations are common in other domains, but, before now, they have not been examined for their relevance to cyberspace. This book examines how strategic A2/AD operations can cut off states from cyberspace through attacks on either the physical or the logic layers of cyberspace. The result of strategic cyber A2/AD operations could be catastrophic for modern economies, governments, military forces, and societies, yet there has been surprisingly little study of these threats to states' access to cyberspace. This book examines the implications of strategic cyber A2/AD operations for deterrence strategy and proposes a new view of how exclusion from cyberspace can be used as a coercive tool in diplomacy.

Alison Lawlor Russell is an assistant professor of political science and international studies at Merrimack College. She is the author of the book *Cyber Blockades* and has written several articles and chapters on cyber strategy and security. Dr. Russell is a nonresident research scientist at the Center for Naval Analyses, the US Department of the Navy's think tank, and holds a PhD from the Fletcher School of Law and Diplomacy at Tufts University. She is a member of the International Studies Association and American Political Science Association.

# Strategic A2/AD in Cyberspace

**ALISON LAWLOR RUSSELL**

Merrimack College

**CAMBRIDGE**
UNIVERSITY PRESS

# CAMBRIDGE
## UNIVERSITY PRESS

University Printing House, Cambridge CB2 8BS, United Kingdom

One Liberty Plaza, 20th Floor, New York, NY 10006, USA

477 Williamstown Road, Port Melbourne, VIC 3207, Australia

4843/24, 2nd Floor, Ansari Road, Daryaganj, Delhi – 110002, India

79 Anson Road, #06–04/06, Singapore 079906

Cambridge University Press is part of the University of Cambridge.

It furthers the University's mission by disseminating knowledge in the pursuit of education, learning, and research at the highest international levels of excellence.

www.cambridge.org
Information on this title: www.cambridge.org/9781107176485
10.1017/9781316817001

First published 2017

*A catalogue record for this publication is available from the British Library.*

*Library of Congress Cataloging-in-Publication Data*
NAMES: Russell, Alison Lawlor, author.
TITLE: Strategic A2/AD in cyberspace / Alison Russell, Merrimack College.
DESCRIPTION: New York, NY : Cambridge University Press, [2017] | Includes bibliographical references and index.
IDENTIFIERS: LCCN 2016041205 | ISBN 9781107176485
SUBJECTS: LCSH: Cyberspace operations (Military science) | Access denial (Military science) | Cyberspace – Security measures. | Cyberterrorism – Prevention.
CLASSIFICATION: LCC U167.5.C92 R87 2017 | DDC 355.4/1–dc23
LC record available at https://lccn.loc.gov/2016041205

ISBN 978-1-107-17648-5 Hardback
ISBN 978-1-316-62962-8 Paperback

*To my children, Catherine, Edward, and Shirin*

# Contents

List of Figures　　　　　　　　　　　　　　　　　　*page* viii

List of Tables　　　　　　　　　　　　　　　　　　　　ix

Acknowledgments　　　　　　　　　　　　　　　　　　x

1　Introduction　　　　　　　　　　　　　　　　　　1

2　Historical Perspective of A2/AD Strategy　　　　　11

3　The Physical Layer　　　　　　　　　　　　　　26

4　The Logic Layer　　　　　　　　　　　　　　　40

5　Implications for Deterrence and Coercion　　　　53

6　Conclusions and Recommendations　　　　　　74

Bibliography　　　　　　　　　　　　　　　　　　83

Index　　　　　　　　　　　　　　　　　　　　　89

# Figures

3.1 Submarine Cable Map from Telegeography     *page* 28

3.2 Intersection of Cyberspace Operations, Electronic Warfare,
and EM Spectrum Management Operations     35

# Tables

3.1  Comparison of Satellites and Submarine Fiber Optic Cables
across Several Key Factors in Telecommunications                *page* 32
4.1  Root Server Names, IP Addresses, and Operators                      42

# Acknowledgments

I must begin by thanking my friend and colleague Colonel Christopher Fitzgerald Wrenn, PhD. The genesis for this book came from a conversation with Chris and a desire to bring together our respective research areas. It was this spark that led the way to the research proposal, funding, and, ultimately, publication of this book. Chris passed away too soon to see the final drafts, but there is no doubt that I would not have written this book without his insights and suggestions. He inspired me to write this book and I hope he would approve of the final result.

I would like to thank the Smith Richardson Foundation for its generous financial support of this research endeavor over the course of two and a half years. The foundation has been incredibly patient and supportive as I met and overcame research hurdles along the way. I would also like to thank the Institute for Foreign Policy Analysis for its institutional support of and enthusiasm for the project, and especially Dr. Bob Pfaltzgraff for his critical engagement with key parts of this book. Thank you also to Professor Joseph Nye for taking the time to talk with me and hash out ideas when this book was still only halfway developed.

There were several conferences, people, and events that motivated me and challenged my work in very productive ways. I would like to thank the US Naval War College, its Symposium on Irregular Warfare and Armed Conflict, and Dr. Andrea Dew, who helped me vet early ideas and get the research off to a solid start. The NATO Cooperative Cyber Defense Centre of Excellence and the 2015 International Conference on Cyber Conflict in Tallinn, Estonia, provided a robust environment for testing draft versions of this work. In particular my conference colleagues Nickolaos Pissanidis, Dr. Steve Chan, Ian Wallace, and others provided a critical examination of the physical layer of cyberspace that made that chapter much stronger. Aditi Desai assisted with the research on the technical aspects of the logic layer. I would like to thank Brian Mazanac, Michael Gerson, and others who provided critical insights and suggestions during the review process; their efforts helped elevate the content of the book.

I would like to thank Admiral Jim Stavridis, USN (retired), for his advice on how to write a book in the real world, when you are big on ideas and short on time. His advice helped me turn blank pages into chapters. Dr. Andy Hess helped me keep the creative part of this endeavor in mind as I churned through the research materials and sought inspiration. Jenifer Burckett-Picker provided invaluable resources at exactly the right time, on multiple occasions; I greatly admire and appreciate her dedication and resourcefulness. Dr. Bill Martel, who always found a way to help me and help others, facilitated the introduction to my editor at Cambridge, John Berger. I will always be grateful to him for that and all of his advice and assistance throughout the years.

I would like to thank Dr. Harry Wessel of the Political Science Department at Merrimack College for supporting this project and advocating for me to have the time necessary to finish the book. I would also like to thank my colleagues at Merrimack College, particularly Dr. Gavril Bilev, Dr. Anne Flaherty, and Dr. He Li, for their support and advice at various stages of the project.

Finally, my family and friends have contributed their talents and efforts to help me keep on track with this project. My parents are sources of endless optimism and encouragement, and my children inspire me to challenge myself. I would especially like to thank my incredible husband Kevin, whose support, patience, and good humor are invaluable to the writing process and my life in general.

# 1

# Introduction

The Information Age of the twenty-first century is distinguished by the proliferation of networks of power that transmit information in a variety of forms and have the effect of defining and decentralizing power relationships. The instantaneous transmission of information through vast geographic space has made possible our current global economic system, as well as the operations of modern governments, militaries, and social organizations. Their capabilities hinge on the accessibility of cyberspace to all participants. To be absent from these networks of information is to be absent from power.[1]

Cyberspace is the modern communications network that underpins global information exchange and services. It is ubiquitous, complex, and much bigger than the Internet alone. It reinforces the global economic order and is essential to all elements of state power, from military operations to electricity to basic communications. Old networks, such as landline-based telephone systems, have been integrated into the newer and more efficient networks of cyberspace. Cyberspace is so ubiquitous that large-scale, strategic connectivity is rarely questioned.

Nevertheless, connectedness to cyberspace should not be taken for granted, especially by states. Cyberspace is a man-made network to which a state can be connected and disconnected, sometimes against its will. Cyber blockades can occur, and states can be denied access to cyberspace.[2] The experience of North Korea in December 2014 illustrated just how quickly and completely a state can be denied access to cyberspace. For nine-and-a-half hours on December 22, North Korea suffered a total outage of Internet connectivity. The event was consistent with a cyber attack, and it came just days after the US Federal Bureau of Investigation said that North Korea was responsible for a major cyber attack on Sony Pictures. However, experts cautioned that North Korea's outage could also be attributed to other causes, such as power problems.[3]

[1] Manuel Castells, *Communication Power* (New York: Oxford University Press, 2009).
[2] Alison Lawlor Russell, *Cyber Blockades* (Washington, DC: Georgetown University Press, 2014).
[3] Chloe Albanesius, "Internet in North Korea Offline after Apparent Attack," *PC Magazine*, December 22, 2014.

Deliberate actions to deny a state access to cyberspace and/or diminish its capacity to operate freely therein may be considered anti-access and area denial operations (or A2/AD operations). According to the modern understanding of A2/AD operations, they specifically mean to deny an adversary the ability to bring its operational capabilities into the contested region or prevent the attacker from operating freely within the region and maximizing its capabilities.[4]

This definition of A2/AD strategy evolved from assessments of anti-access warfare strategies in other domains – that is, on land, at sea, and in the air. The US Department of Defense (DoD) has designated cyberspace as "an operational domain … to operate and defend its networks, and to organize, train, and equip [its] forces to perform cyber missions."[5] Therefore, it is appropriate and prudent to investigate the extension of strategies, such as A2/AD from the other domains to cyberspace.[6]

As a side note, the White House has also emphasized repeatedly that cyberspace is much more than an operational domain and should not be militarized or portrayed as such. Deputy Secretary of Defense William J. Lynn III noted that DoD's cyber strategy's

> emphasis on cyber defenses illustrates how we are both mindful of those who would do us harm using cyber means, but also committed to protecting the peaceful use of cyberspace. Far from "militarizing" cyberspace, our strategy of securing networks to deny the benefit of an attack will help dissuade military actors from using cyberspace for hostile purposes. Indeed, establishing robust cyber defenses no more militarizes cyberspace than having a navy militarizes the ocean. This commitment to peace through preventive defense is at the heart of our DoD Cyber Strategy and the Administration's overall approach to cyberspace.[7]

### ANTI-ACCESS WARFARE

A2/AD operations include a variety of military activities that can occur in multiple domains (i.e., land, sea, and air). Traditionally, A2/AD activities have been designed

4  Sam J. Tangredi, *Anti-Access Warfare: Countering A2/AD Strategies* (Annapolis, MD: Naval Institute Press, 2013), 1–2.
5  William J. Lynn, "Deputy Secretary of Defense Speech: Remarks on the Department of Defense Cyber Strategy," news release, July 14, 2011, http://archive.defense.gov/speeches/speech.aspx?speechid=1593.
6  Cyberspace differs from the other domains in three important ways. First, the other domains would exist without human action. Cyberspace was created by humans and will cease to exist and function without continued human interaction and upkeep. Second, cyberspace traverses the other domains. Fiber optic cables run along the sea floor, satellites transmit information, and wireless signals fly through the air. The other domains touch, but do not rely on each other in the same way that cyberspace relies on the other domains. Third, the topography of cyberspace is constantly changing and being modified by human interaction. As the terrain is constantly changing, it is especially difficult to protect and defend against attacks.
7  Lynn, "Deputy Secretary of Defense Speech."

to establish and maintain control of the battle space – an objective of any military force. The goal is to deny the adversary the ability to enter the area and maneuver freely within the battle space. Anti-access and area denial are different but related concepts that offer a nuanced approach to deny the adversary the ability to operate within a contested zone.

"Anti-access" traditionally refers to the ability to cordon off an area and control entry to it, thus effectively denying the adversary entry to the contested area. A naval blockade is an example of an anti-access operation because it prevents external access to a particular area but does not necessarily control what occurs within that area. Area denial refers to the ability to diminish, degrade, or destroy the adversary's freedom of action within the contested area. A no-fly zone that neutralizes aircraft within a specific area is a form of area denial. In short, anti-access affects movement *to* a theater, while AD anti-denial affects movement *within* a theater.

A2/AD strategy is a contingency for which states could plan *for* and *against*. In some cases, a state seeks to employ A2/AD strategies against an adversary, while in other cases, an adversary may try to use an A2/AD strategy against it. Within the US military and policy community, A2/AD operations are also commonly associated with the Joint Concept for Access and Maneuver in the Global Commons and other joint operations. The primary difference between these two concepts is that US policy considers A2/AD operations something that it must defend against, whereas "Joint Concept for Access and Maneuver in the Global Commons" is the term used to describe similar actions that are taken offensively by the United States.[8] Both of these strategies focus on joint operations in the other domains; however, they are also applicable to the cyber domain, where access is a necessary precondition to being able to operate from any distance.

## A2/AD OPERATIONS IN CYBERSPACE

The concept of A2/AD operations as it pertains to cyberspace is an evolving concept in warfare. Most of the extant literature about anti-access warfare or A2/AD strategies focuses on what has been done historically on land, at sea, and in the air and what is being discussed now regarding US military planning for future threats, specifically those that might emanate from Asia.[9] Information and communications has long been considered as a key to victory or defeat in conflict, whether it was Sun Tzu's emphasis on intelligence gathering and deception or, more recently, decision-making

---

[8] This distinction is discussed at length in Chapter 2.
[9] There is a dearth of scholarly literature on anti-access warfare, with the notable exception of Sam J. Tangredi's book *Anti-Access Warfare*, while the media and government reports on the subject tend to focus on the specifics of current military planning. Discussions of anti-access warfare and cyberspace in any of the literature are rare and usually quite limited.

theories such as Boyd's OODA loop theory that emphasizes perceptions, environment, culture, and analysis.[10] A2/AD operations in cyberspace do not seek to manipulate the information, but rather seek to disrupt and prevent the flow or exchange of information.

The capability to conduct A2/AD operations in cyberspace, or "cyber A2/AD," exists on two levels. At the tactical level, cyberspace can be used as an avenue for conducting cyber attacks that will result in A2/AD operations in other domains. For example, sophisticated cyber attacks may be designed to destroy specific satellite imagery capabilities, missile targeting, or even navigational equipment to facilitate A2/AD operations at sea or in the air.[11] This level of cyber A2/AD is commonly discussed and relatively well known by operational planners and cyber tactical teams.[12]

At the strategic level, cyber A2/AD receives very little attention and is relatively underexamined by scholars and policy makers. These strategic A2/AD operations in cyberspace are the target of this book. Strategic cyber A2/AD operations are defined here as the ability to gain control of the network or infrastructure of cyberspace and manipulate it in such a way as to deny a state the ability to use cyberspace *in any capacity*. Unlike tactical cyber A2/AD operations, it does not target the functionality of specific weapons or information systems that are connected to cyberspace, but rather targets states' access to the grid itself.[13]

A2/AD operations in cyberspace are of significant and increasing concern for US national security. In the Joint Operation Access Concept of 2012, the US DoD identified three trends that directly led to the increase of A2/AD capabilities around the world in recent years. One of these trends is the *"emergence of space and cyberspace as increasingly important and contested domains"* (emphasis added) as a factor affecting the rise of A2/AD threats. In addition to proliferation of advanced technologies and changing US defensive posture, the proliferation of and dependence on cyberspace is a leading factor in the A2/AD vulnerability.[14] Furthermore,

[10]   OODA stands for "observe, orient, decide, act," and it refers to the decision-making cycle developed by Col. John Boyd, USAF. For more information, see Frans P. B. Osinga, *Science, Strategy and War: The Strategic Theory of John Boyd*, Strategy and History (London; New York: Routledge, 2007).

[11]   Harry Kazianis, "The Real Anti-Access Story: Cyber" *Flashpoints: Diplomacy by Other Means* (2013), http://thediplomat.com/flashpoints-blog/2013/05/15/the-real-anti-access-story-cyber/; Nathan Freier, "The Emerging Anti-Access/Area-Denial Challenge" (Center for Strategic and International Studies, May 17, 2012).

[12]   For more information on the application of operational cyber A2/AD in naval strategy and security, see Alison Lawlor Russell, "Cyber and Naval Strategy" in *Routledge Handbook of Naval Strategy and Security*, ed. Joachim Krause and Sebastian Bruns (Routledge, 2015), 189–201.

[13]   This definition specifically focuses on denying *states* the ability to access cyberspace. Non-state actors are exceedingly important actors in the international system and particularly in cyberspace, but anti-access warfare strategies have long been the purview of states, city-states, empires, and other recognized political entities that control territory and raise armed forces. The effort to keep individuals and groups out of cyberspace would more likely fall into the realm of law enforcement and domestic control, as opposed to military operations and international relations.

[14]   U.S. Department of Defense, "Joint Operational Access Concept" (2012), ii.

one of the main precepts identified for achieving operational access in the face of armed opposition is to "protect space and cyber assets while attacking the enemy's cyber and space capabilities."[15] As the DoD attempts to address A2/AD threats and opportunities, academics, scholars, and policy makers must come to a greater understanding of how cyberspace works in order to protect US access and potentially deny it to adversaries.

### Layers and Vulnerabilities for Strategic Cyber A2/AD Operations

Given the structure of cyberspace, there are multiple ways by which strategic A2/AD operations can be achieved in that domain. Cyberspace is a global grid that can be manipulated, expanded, and contracted to increase or decrease accessibility. It is comprised of multiple layers, which means that there are different types of vulnerabilities inherent in cyber A2/AD, depending on the layer of cyberspace. Most scholars agree that there are four layers to cyberspace: the physical foundations, the logic layer, the information layer, and the users.[16]

The physical layer of cyberspace is comprised of physical elements, from satellites to fiber optic cables and cell towers, to computers and servers. Of chief importance are the fiber optic cables that traverse the globe and transmit data packages from one location to another. In addition to these cables, there are physical nodes of cables (where cables come together) and server farms that centralize the processing of data packages and route them to their final destination. Also, of significant importance, particularly for government and military operations, are the satellites that provide connectivity to remote areas.

The chief vulnerabilities in the physical layer lie with the cables themselves. Most cables are located undersea and lie on the seabed floor. These cables are unprotected and can be damaged by accident or malicious intent. Furthermore, there are only a handful of ships worldwide that are capable of repairing fiber optic cables, and their schedules are booked years in advance, making repair of cables a challenging task. Fortunately, the cables are somewhat geographically dispersed because they connect different cities and regions. However, they come together at cable landing sites. These cable landing sites are single points of risk, where cables come together to make landfall in a region.[17] Physical damage to the cables at the landing sites is possible; despite their importance to the functionality of cyberspace, they are usually

---

[15] Ibid., iii.
[16] Gregory J. Rattray, *Strategic Warfare in Cyberspace* (Cambridge, MA: MIT Press, 2001); Nazli Choucri and David D. Clark, "Integrating Cyberspace and International Relations: The Co-Evolution Dilemma," in *ECIR Workshop on Who Controls Cyberspace?* (Explorations in Cyber International Relations, Harvard University and Massachusetts Institute for Technology, 2012).
[17] Michael Sechrist, "New Threats, Old Technology: Vulnerabilities in Undersea Communications Cable Network Management Systems," in *Science, Technology, & Public Policy Program Discussion Paper Series* (Cambridge, MA: Explorations in Cyber International Relations Project at Belfer Center for Science and International Affairs, 2012), 10.

unmarked, unprotected locations with little to no physical security. For example, nearly all of the trans-Atlantic cables for the United States come ashore near New York City and are consolidated in a pipe that runs under a building in lower Manhattan.[18]

The logic layer is the central nervous system of cyberspace; it is responsible for routing data packages to their final destinations, primarily via domain name systems (DNS), Internet protocols, browsers, Web sites, and software, all of which rely on the aforementioned fiber optic cables and physical foundations. Targeted cyber attacks can manipulate the logic layer of cyberspace in a number of ways, causing it to malfunction or shut down completely in order to inhibit the flow of data. For this reason, there are some safeguards in place to diminish the risk of cyber attacks that target these systems, including redundancies and the ability to reroute traffic through an uncompromised server. For example, all thirteen of the Internet root servers were attacked simultaneously in 2002. Several servers were able to withstand the attack and continued to operate, thus keeping the Internet functioning despite the fact that several servers were temporarily shut down by the attack.[19] Despite this attack over a decade ago, vulnerabilities still exist and can be exploited. Chief among them are the operating systems that manage the wavelengths of the fiber optic cables as they come ashore at landing sites. Using these systems, hackers could manipulate the wavelengths to alter or remove some or all of the data traffic on that cable, potentially without the operator's knowledge.[20]

This threat is reminiscent of Stuxnet in that a computer worm was able to manipulate the inner workings of advanced technology equipment while simultaneously masking its effects to the system's operator. Compounding the threat is the fact that the network management systems for the cables use a supervisory control and data acquisition system (SCADA) that is both a Windows operating system and connected to the Internet. The Windows operating system has significant and well-known vulnerabilities, and by connecting to the Internet, the system is more accessible to hackers who seek to do harm (unlike Stuxnet, which was not connected to the Internet yet was able to access the SCADA system anyway).[21]

The information layer, which consists of codes, text, photos, and other materials that are stored or transmitted through cyberspace and the user layer, can also be targeted for attack, but it would be significantly more difficult to achieve strategic A2/AD effects by targeting these layers. Attacks at these levels involve so many variables and discrete targets that it would make it incredibly impractical and likely ineffective to attempt strategic A2/AD operations by targeting the information or user layers, unless it were for the purpose of information campaigns or psychological operations.

---

[18]   Ibid., 9.   [19]   "Internet Backbone Withstands Major Attack," *MacWorld.com*, October 23, 2002.
[20]   Sechrist, "New Threats, Old Technology," 12.   [21]   Ibid., 13.

In addition to the four layers of cyberspace, there are three distinct types of attacks that could occur in cyberspace. First, there are mechanical attacks, such as the bombing of command-and-control centers or cutting of cables. These are not common but are entirely possible and plausible types of attack, particularly in wartime. Next are attacks within the electromagnetic spectrum, including electromagnetic pulses (EMP) or jamming of frequencies. Finally, the most common types of attacks in cyberspace are digital attacks, such as intrusion of systems and networks.[22]

These types of attacks overlap with the layers of cyberspace, to a certain extent. The physical attacks must target the physical infrastructure, of course, but digital attacks could target the logic layer or the informational layer of cyberspace. Electromagnetic attacks would fall between the physical layer and the logic layer, as they would target the physical (but invisible) wavelengths that transmit data. Thus, to maintain full operational capacity of cyberspace, the electromagnetic spectrum, physical layer, and logic layer must be protected.[23]

A strategic cyber A2/AD attack would likely focus on the physical and logic layers of the Internet because they are the backbone and nervous system of the system; take down either one of these, and you can take down the whole network. In order to understand the vulnerabilities of cyberspace to a strategic A2/AD attack, it is necessary to go beyond the technical description of the environment and discuss who controls these layers and, thereby, the entire system of cyberspace. Who controls cyberspace and influences its development are important questions when considering the system's ability to withstand pressure, manipulation, and coercion and the need for cooperation among multiple stakeholders. Unlike other domains or the global commons, such as air, land, and sea, cyberspace is predominantly man-made. As a result, interaction with human beings is critical to the functioning of the domain, even while this feature opens up new avenues of possible vulnerabilities for the domain. The major actors who have power over various points of control over cyberspace include cable owners and maintenance companies, Internet service providers (ISPs), server systems including DNS, and operating systems, among others.[24]

There are many questions that derive from this research that are of great importance for states in the modern era with advanced technologies, many of which are cyber dependent. The primary questions that arise are, how vulnerable are states to strategic A2/AD operations in cyberspace, and how can states increase their own security and minimize the vulnerabilities that others may try to exploit? Beyond these questions of immediate security, the implications of cyber A2/AD operations are broad and affect many aspects of planning and policy. Can denial of access be

---

[22] Rattray, *Strategic Warfare in Cyberspace*, 17–32.
[23] U.S. Department of Defense, "Joint Operational Access Concept," 26.
[24] David Clark, *Control Point Analysis* (Cambridge, MA: Massachusetts Institute of Technology, 2012), 13.

a form of punitive sanction for rogue regimes that behave outside of the boundaries of international norms? Can the threat of denial of access act be a credible form of deterrence? What are the advantages and limitations of such a strategy? What are the appropriate roles of states and private corporations with regard to strategic A2/AD operations in cyberspace? Is cyberspace center of gravity for the modern era?

The questions of deterrence, coercion, and centers of gravity are particularly important for strategic A2/AD operations in cyberspace. Given the extensive reliance of modern states and societies on cyberspace, the ability to deny access to cyberspace would threaten the economy, security, and stability of a state. A credible threat of this nature may be sufficient to deter armed conflict or compel a more favorable course of action. Thus, strategic A2/AD operations in cyberspace may create new options in the panoply of tools for international relations.

## Gaps in Knowledge

The gaps in knowledge with regard to strategic A2/AD operations in cyberspace are vast. Specifically, policy makers need to know how A2/AD operations apply to cyberspace in a strategic manner, as well as the implications of this for national security. The DoD report *Joint Operation Access Concept* of 2012 was the first major report or article to bring this specific issue into the public discussion. However, most scholarly and policy articles continue to address the questions of conducting operations within the domain, not as a means of securing access or denying other actors access to cyberspace in its entirety.

There exist possibly a few reasons for this gap. First, the study of cyberspace and cyber security is a new and quickly growing field that strives to cover myriad issues and problems posed by a dynamic and unique invention that has fundamentally changed many aspects of life. This evolution in technology has had profound consequences that researchers and policy makers are still striving to understand and address.

Second, digital cyber attacks are occurring all the time and can cause serious damage to financial, government, and defense industries. Digital cyber attacks receive a significant amount of attention because of the sheer volume of attacks that occur daily. However, while some digital attacks can be severe and costly, the majority are mere nuisances designed to harass Web site owners or users or convey political or social messages.

Third, there appears to be a reluctance to discuss the possibility of catastrophic failure or denial of access to cyberspace. The system was designed to be redundant and resilient to maximize its ability to withstand major attacks on key nodes of communication. However, redundancy and resiliency should not be taken for granted when millions of users depend on this technology for essential activities in all parts of life. Cyberspace is comprised of both physical and digital elements, both of which can be manipulated, damaged, or destroyed to change the topography of the domain and render it inaccessible to some or all users.

This research attempts to fill specific critical gaps in academics' and policy makers' knowledge and expertise. Specifically, it seeks to demonstrate how strategic A2/AD activities are relevant for cyberspace, which has not been sufficiently addressed in the scholarly or policy literature. To do so, it will assess the vulnerabilities and opportunities for strategic A2/AD operations at the physical and logic layers of cyberspace.

In addition, this book seeks to address how strategic A2/AD operations in cyberspace can provide a new instrument for coercion, sanction, and deterrence in the international community. It links strategic A2/AD operations in cyberspace to deterrence theory, a necessary endeavor because current debate and literature on cyber deterrence do not account for strategic A2/AD in cyberspace.

As the United States is at the forefront of the development of cyberspace and cyber security, it is in a position to benefit the most from this type of research and analysis. This research hopes to shed light on the ways that policy makers can use strategic cyber A2/AD operations to pursue the national interest and advance foreign policy goals, and scholars can incorporate emergent technologic capabilities into existing security paradigms.

## RESEARCH QUESTIONS AND ORGANIZATION OF THE BOOK

The driving questions to be addressed through this research are as follows:

1. How do A2/AD operations apply to cyberspace in a strategic manner?
2. What are the implications of this for academics, researchers, policy makers, and national security in general?

Historical review in Chapter 2 will examine the evolution of A2/AD operations in other domains to elucidate how they have been employed and to what degree of success. It also examines the evolution of current US strategy for A2/AD and policies on cyberspace. Next, the research applies this understanding of A2/AD operations to cyberspace. In Chapters 3 and 4, it examines strategic A2/AD with regard to the physical aspects of cyberspace (i.e., cables, satellites) and the logic layer (i.e., servers, routing, nodes, and hubs) including strengths, weaknesses, opportunities, and threats of each. As discussed above, these are the layers of cyberspace that are most likely to be targeted for a strategic cyber A2/AD attack, so the research addresses how an attack could occur and the effects that an attack could have. This research investigates how cyberspace is physically and digitally constructed and determines its key nodes and access points. It attempts to identify who owns or controls these access points, whether they be government or private sector actors. The research is focused on strategy and policy but also incorporates some technical assessments in order to illustrate how the key nodes and access points to cyberspace could be compromised and what the ramification of this would be for the United States or another country.

After the discussion of how strategic A2/AD operations could be conducted in cyberspace, Chapter 5 explores the potential effects of these operations and the policy implications for states. Strategic cyber A2/AD affects deterrence strategy in particular, as well as the related efforts of coercion and sanctions. Therefore, the main questions to be addressed here include the following: Can strategic cyber A2/AD operations be a credible form of deterrence? How does this relate to traditional deterrence strategy? What are the advantages and limitations of strategic cyber A2/AD as a deterrent? Is cyberspace a new center of gravity and, if so, what are the implications of this? Finally, in Chapter 6, the analysis of the implications of strategic A2/AD operations in cyberspace, conclusions, and recommendations are intended to generate discussion among scholars, policy makers, and military planners.

## 2

# Historical Perspective of A2/AD Strategy

Written records of anti-access warfare strategies date back to 480 BC, when the independent city-states of Greece were menaced by the Persian emperor Xerxes and the largest armed force ever assembled at that time.[1] According to the historian Herodotus, Xerxes' forces included 1.7 million troops and 1,327 warships (although the number of troops was, in all likelihood, much smaller; the larger number may have included warriors as well as camp followers). In contrast, the Greek city-states each had only a few thousand defenders and had rarely before been united.[2]

The weaker Greek city-states were able to defeat Xerxes and his great army by pursuing a strategy of anti-access. The Greek islands provided natural barriers and chokepoints that the Greeks used to their advantage to destroy or cut off critical supply and logistic lines. By preventing the necessary supply ships from reaching the soldiers ashore, the Greeks turned Xerxes' strength into a weakness: His army was too big to live off the land and could not survive without shipments of grain, which could only be brought by sea. The Spartan rulers convincingly bluffed that more Greek forces were on the way and that Xerxes had limited time to save himself and his troops before they would be cut down by the approaching Greek warriors. Xerxes retreated to Asia and left behind a contingent of 20,000 troops, which suffered from starvation and desertion, and was eventually destroyed by the Greek warriors.[3]

The largest army the world had ever known at that point in history was denied access by a much smaller force, and the mighty Xerxes forfeited his goal of conquering all of Greece. Instead of achieving victory, he was forced to retreat. In this case, the power of the anti-access strategy was that it allowed the weaker force to prevent the stronger force from bringing its resources to bear in the theater of operations; in other words, it neutralized the superior force and then waited for time, attrition, and/or extrinsic events to shake the determination of the attacker or change the cost–benefit calculation.[4] Sun Tzu said it is better to

---

[1]  For a detailed historical analysis of anti-access warfare, see Tangredi, *Anti-Access Warfare*.
[2]  Ibid., 7–8.    [3]  Ibid., 7–10.    [4]  Ibid., 8–15.

never fight the enemy at all, but rather to be victorious without a battle. Anti-access and area denial, or A2/AD, strategies can defeat an enemy with minimal fighting.

Geography often provides some of the greatest strategic buffer zones and can be a decisive factor in A2/AD strategies. As famously noted by Sir Eyre Crowe, "the immutable circumstances of geography" protected England from many continental adversaries.[5] Likewise, the United States has benefited tremendously from the vast oceans that buffered it from European and Asian conflicts and made it much more secure against adversaries. Specific geography is not a necessary component of an A2/AD strategy, but it has been undeniably helpful for A2/AD operations on land and sea as geographical chokepoints and difficult terrain provide favorable opportunities for A2/AD operations.

A cornerstone of US national security policy is the ability to project power globally. A2/AD strategies, when employed by adversarial countries and in contradiction to international law, threaten that capability. A2/AD is a defensive strategy, as it seeks to prevent both access to an area and maneuverability within it. Counter-A2/AD is the offensive strategy employed by forces seeking to break through an A2/AD strategy in order to gain access to strategic locations or, in some cases, uphold international law, such as the freedom of navigation guaranteed under the United Nations Convention on the Law of the Sea. Whether A2/AD strategies are "good" or "bad" depends entirely on perspective and goals; they are merely tools at the disposal of strategists.

WHO ENGAGES IN A2/AD?

A2/AD strategies can be employed by any state, but they are particularly attractive when geography and/or political circumstances support them and when the force implementing an A2/AD strategy is a strategically weaker force and thus would not be able to defeat the adversary in a head-to-head competition. That said, strategically and militarily strong states have successfully employed A2/AD strategies many times throughout history; they are not solely strategies of the weak. The "advantage" of this strategy is that one does not have to be the strongest force to win – one just has to be strong enough to keep the other force from gaining access to that which they seek to conquer. Usually, military forces seek to defeat strategic assets or destroy important targets; thus if the defending force can defend these targets from a greater distance away – potentially in a location where the geography is advantageous to defense – that force may be able to decrease the likelihood of the aggressor succeeding in reaching its target.

---

[5]  Eyre Crowe, "Memorandum on the Present State of British Relations with France and Germany" (London, 1907).

## A2/AD IN THE MARITIME DOMAIN

A2/AD has a long tradition in the maritime domain, which affords many geographical advantages for A2/AD strategies. For example, the geographic isolation of islands and the presence of chokepoints such as inlets, isthmuses, straits, and other nautical features lend themselves well to anti-access measures and make it easier to implement area denial strategies. It is instructive that when the Greek city-states fought off the great army of Xerxes, it was the islands that provided natural barriers and straits that the Greeks could use to their advantage to cut off critical supply and logistic lines. Likewise, the Strait of Hormuz in the Persian Gulf is a chokepoint for a significant portion of the world's oil, but also for the maritime forces of Iraq, Kuwait, Bahrain, Qatar, the United Arab Emirates, and Iran. An anti-access strategy is easiest to implement when there are limited ways to reach the target under the best circumstances.

Naval history has a long tradition of A2/AD operations, although they typically appeared under different names, such as "power projection," "sea control," "command of the seas," and "blockades." In the late nineteenth century, Sir Alfred T. Mahan, naval officer and strategist, wrote about the importance of maritime forces to the strength of a nation. A dominant navy that commands the sea could not only defeat other navies but also control international trade – of particular importance in the 1890s during an early but prominent phase of globalization. The ability to control the sea lines of communication (SLOCs) and dominate the maritime domain gave nations an advantage in global commerce and trade. Thus, whoever controls the SLOCs commands the trade and commerce of other nations. Command of the seas, or "sea control," as it came to be called, was essential for the overall strength and power of a nation, on land as well as at sea.[6]

Naval blockades are the quintessential anti-access operation. The goal of these blockades is to cut off access to and from a specific geographic area. The blockade applies to all parties and maritime traffic, whether for commercial or military endeavors. Naval area denial operations often go by the name "sea control," which places emphasis on dominating the area of operation and degrading or restricting the capabilities that can be brought to bear by adversarial forces in the region. Power projection capabilities reflect the essence of Mahan's strategy: the ability to project maritime power to anywhere on the globe, including in order to be able to counter A2/AD measures undertaken by other forces that may want to restrict movement near their territorial waters or, conversely, to impose those conditions on adversaries in order to limit their ability to use the full spectrum of capabilities.[7]

---

[6]  Alfred Thayer Mahan, *The Influence of Sea Power upon History, 1660–1783*, 6th edn. (Boston: Little, Brown, and Company, 1894).

[7]  The United Nations Convention on the Law of the Sea (UNCLOS) states that every country has a 12-nautical-mile area of territorial water off of its coast and up to 200 miles of exclusive economic zone.

## A2/AD ON LAND

A2/AD strategies can be employed on land as well. Whether it is impassable mountain roads, bodies of water, or climate that makes terrain inaccessible, there are natural features that can make some A2/AD operations inherently more likely to succeed than others. Man-made constructs, such as bridges, can also support anti-access operations. The concept is the same as in the other domains: One side seeks to prevent the other side from gaining access to an area or theater of operations by closing off access to that theater. If access cannot be completely thwarted, then area denial operations occur when one side seeks to degrade the capabilities of the other and defeat it in a battle. Anti-access can apply to the fighting forces directly (keep the warfighters out) or to the logistics and supply trains that support the warfighters, thereby degrading their supplies and capabilities, and adopting a strategy of "waiting out" the battle until the side without replenishments is sufficiently weakened and must surrender, must retreat, or can be defeated more easily. This strategy was employed by the Greek city-states against Xerxes' large army, which eventually capitulated when faced with serious hunger and mass desertion within the ranks.

Area denial operations on land are very similar to guerrilla warfare or an insurgency. The objectives of both are to prevent the enemy from bringing its full capability and capacity to bear, and the methods to achieve this typically include indirect and harassing fires, operational maneuver, deception, and strike-move-hide tactics so as to avoid direct confrontation with and prevent the adversary from using its capabilities in an ideal manner.[8] In both area denial and guerrilla warfare, one force is not able to prevent the other side from gaining entry, but it can undertake operations to degrade the adversary's ability to use its capabilities as intended or to maximize its abilities.

On land as well, geography can be a natural barrier that protects countries, making anti-access strategies more successful. Islands are naturally isolated, and mountains can impede invading forces. Terrain that becomes impassable in certain weather, such as with floods or snow, also can facilitate an anti-access or area denial strategy. Although it was Russian forces that defeated Napoleon's army on the fatal march toward Moscow in 1812, the cold, harsh winter, agonizing cold, exhaustion, and lack of supplies rendered Napoleon's troops vulnerable and tipped the balance in favor of the Russian Army.

## A2/AD IN THE AIR

A2/AD in the air differs from that in the maritime domain or on land because air lacks geographical features that provide natural boundaries or helpful delineations. Nonetheless, A2/AD operations in the air are fairly well known but go by a different

---

[8]  Tangredi, *Anti-Access Warfare*, 69.

name: no-fly zones. These are military operations that cordon off part of the airspace and prohibit the entrance and exit for all aircraft, except for those that have been specifically approved, such as friendly forces or humanitarian relief. The anti-access part of a no-fly zone is the cordoning off of the air with an international announcement that a no-fly zone will be established there. The area denial part of the operation is what occurs if or when an aircraft violates the no-fly zone and enters the restricted space. There are a number of options employed by the imposer of these zones. The intruding aircraft can be ordered to leave the airspace immediately, fighter jets can scramble to accompany the aircraft and escort it out of airspace, jets can try to force the plane to land, and, as a last resort, the intruding aircraft can be shot down.

No-fly zones can be imposed for a number of reasons: as a part of a military operation to ensure the safety of friendly forces on the ground and prevent hostile attacks (such as the Israeli aerial blockade of Lebanon in 2006), as a tool of coercion to induce changes in behaviors (such as Operations Southern Watch and Northern Watch over Iraq in the 1990s), and as a humanitarian effort to protect people on the ground from air assault by an oppressive or hostile regime (such as Operation Deny Flight over Bosnia from 1993 to 1995 or in Libya in 2011). No-fly zones can be implemented by a single state with the capacity and will to do so, or they can come as part of a broader multinational or international effort, such as the no-fly zones in Iraq, Bosnia, and Libya.

The ultimate goal of a no-fly zone is to reduce the capabilities of the target state by establishing air dominance in order to achieve political objectives on the ground, whether they involve kinetic targeting, humanitarian relief, or policy changes. Although no-fly zones focus on cordoning off an area in the air to prevent the entrance or exit of aircraft, they also involve the destruction of land-based sensors and weaponry, such as navigational equipment or anti-aircraft missiles. Thus, A2/AD operations in the air cannot be confined solely to targets in that space, but also necessitate the removal of supporting equipment and potential threats to aircraft that are land based or sea based.

## LIMITATIONS OF A2/AD STRATEGIES

A2/AD strategies have their limitations, as all strategies do. As a strategy for achieving victory or dominance, A2/AD strategies can assist in pinning down adversarial forces and denying them entry, but A2/AD strategies alone will not defeat an enemy. For an enemy to be defeated, other events need to take place. These could be other military campaigns to destroy enemy forces, exogenous international political events that require the adversary to redirect its focus, economic crises that undermine the adversary's ability to support its forces in the theater, or a significant domestic event that requires a response or reprioritization of resources and political capital. For nondemocratic countries whose primary goal is to remain in control over society, a significant domestic event that challenges the status quo would result in a change in other polities in order to maintain regime control. International political events could also necessitate change, but they would have to be of sufficient importance or urgency for the regime to justify the change. Some regimes are more sensitive to economic crisis than others, but certainly a significant crisis would force a reconsideration, if not reformulation, of strategy.

## CURRENT US POLICY ON A2/AD OPERATIONS

While anti-access and area denial operations have a long history, they have taken on new meaning and importance in US policy since the end of the Cold War. After the Cold War, the US military reoriented its strategy to account for a more diverse set of challenges, most notably rogue states and non-state actors that favored asymmetric warfare and the vulnerability of US forces stationed abroad and at forward operating bases. Foreign bases were key to the US ability to project force into far-flung areas of the world, yet because of their importance, they were the logical place for adversaries to attack in order to stymie US intervention in a region. As a result, US strategy began to focus on potential anti-access and area denial operations that could be used to keep US forces out of a contested area, or limit US ability to effectively leverage forces in place.

The US policy perspective of A2/AD strategy is that it is a weapon of the weaker forcer that would be used against the US military. US concerns about A2/AD strategies originated with the perspective of rogue states and non-state actors seeking to use A2/AD operations against the United States, and policy makers have maintained this perspective through the subsequent development of A2/AD policy and strategy. The US government sees itself as the superior force that is being countered with an A2/AD strategy; however, this is a US policy choice with regard to the terminology and characterization of A2/AD as a weapon of the weak. There is no practical reason why the United States cannot use this strategy against an adversary. The fundamentals of an A2/AD strategy are such that it is not exclusively a weapon of the weak; it can be employed effectively by either party in a conflict.

The US policy community refers to counter-A2/AD operations as the Joint Concept for Access and Maneuver in the Global Commons (formerly Air Sea Battle).[9] However, the principles for the Joint Concept and A2/AD are essentially the same; the main difference is one of position: Is the United States in an offensive or defensive position? This distinction is important to policy makers and strategists, and is worth clarifying at the outset, so as to avoid confusion. The emphasis of this research is on the strategy of A2/AD and understanding how it can be used by or against an adversary, not on the specific US policy construct of A2/AD as a weapon of the weak.

[9]   Norton A. Schwartz and Jonathan W. Greenert, "Air-Sea Battle," *The American Interest* (2012).

In a 2002 report for the Center for Strategic and Budgetary Assessments called "The Challenge of Maritime Transformation: Is Bigger Better?," Robert O. Work introduced the idea of anti-access networks that described a potential adversary's overarching system of electronic measures and countermeasures, sensors, and offensive and defensive weaponry that could be employed in support of an anti-access strategy, specifically to "deter, prevent, or disrupt U.S. movement into a theater."[10] As a retired marine colonel and subsequent undersecretary of the Navy, Work was writing about naval capabilities in general and not cyberspace specifically, but cyberspace is the quintessential system of systems, network of networks. Thus, as Sam Tangredi points out, "viewing the anti-access efforts as a network of strategies, techniques, and systems prompts the understanding that defeat of a particular portion of the network could seriously degrade it. Likewise, it points to the need for redundancy in systems and fallback strategies in order to deal with critical damage."[11] Work repeatedly points out that in order to effectively counter A2/AD strategies, the United States would need to employ a joint approach that included, at a minimum, air and naval forces.

One year later, in a 2003 report for the Center for Strategic and Budgetary Assessments called "Meeting the Anti-Access and Area Denial Challenge," Andrew Krepinevich, Barry Watts, and Robert O. Work drew attention to the joint nature of the A2/AD challenge. In it they described anti-access efforts as a network because the strategy must coordinate all elements of joint power to prevent any gaps or seams on land, in the air, or at sea that the enemy can exploit. Citing political, geographic, and resource constraints, the authors note that power-project capabilities are becoming more difficult. Adversaries have had the opportunity to study how the US military operates and deploys its forces, and thus create counterstrategies for use in the event of a conflict. This report cites a retired Indian brigadier general who observed that access to forward operating bases

> is, by far the trickiest part of the American operational problem. This is the proverbial "Achilles heel." India needs to study the vulnerabilities and create covert bodies to develop plans and execute operations to degrade these facilities in the run up to and after commencement of hostilities. Scope exists for low cost options to significantly reduce the combat potential of forces operating from these facilities.[12]

Enemies or potential enemies might employ a variety of methods, from political to geographic to informational to military strategies, in order to deny access to a region

---

[10]  Robert O. Work, *The Challenge of Maritime Transformation: Is Bigger Better?* (Washington, DC: Center for Strategic and Budgetary Assessment, 2002), 10.

[11]  Tangredi, *Anti-Access Warfare*, 50, 63.

[12]  Andrew Krepinevich, Barry Watts, and Robert Work, *Meeting the Anti-Access and Area-Denial Challenge* (Washington, DC: Center for Strategic and Budgetary Assessments, 2003), 4; Referencing Brigadier V. K. Nair, *War in the Gulf: Lessons for the Third World* (New Delhi, India: Lancer International, 1992), 230.

or degrade the effectiveness of forces within that region. These strategies may include the following:

- Political access denial (achieved by entering into alliances with neighbors, or threatening to attack them, in order to deny access to US forces)
- Geographic access denial (stressing US forces' range and targeting capabilities by deploying forces far inland)
- Hardening of fixed targets (such as command centers, leadership facilities, or WMD facilities)
- Creation of sanctuaries (either technically through employment of local global positioning systems jamming or through asymmetric tactics such as hiding among civilian populations or near cultural, historic, or religious landmarks)
- Information operation attacks against US networks, particularly those that are involved with the flow of forces into the region
- Unconventional attacks against critical junctures, such as transshipment points and places of embarkation and debarkation of forces.[13]

In this report, Krepinevich, Watts, and Work coined the term "A2/AD" to describe the threats posed by long-range missile systems, precision munitions, and satellite technology that will make military operations in the littoral areas challenging for modern naval forces. While the term was relatively new, the idea behind it was familiar. Military forces have always strived to develop progressively longer-range weapons systems and capabilities that may give them an advantage over their enemies while keeping their own troops at a safer distance. Whether it is in the form of longer-range guns, intercontinental ballistic missiles, or unmanned vehicles, there is an obvious appeal to be able to fight from a distance.[14]

In 2009 the Navy and Air Force began developing the Air Sea Battle (ASB) concept (formalized in February 2010), which was designed to help combatant commanders integrate the forces at their disposal in order to achieve desired effects in countering emerging A2/AD threats. This concept took into consideration threats that included capabilities such as guided missiles, submarines, sea mines, and cyber weapons that could be used to deny the United States access to contested areas. The ABS concept grew out of a need to reinvigorate skill sets that may have atrophied during the wars in Iraq and Afghanistan, where other skills were more critical to mission success, as well as a recognition that a strategic pivot toward East Asia, and China in particular, may require more robust counter-A2/AD strategies.[15]

---

[13] Krepinevich, Watts, and Work, "Meeting the Anti-Access and Area-Denial Challenge," 6–7.
[14] LCDR Benjamin "BJ" Armstrong, "A2/AD, WWATMD?," *U.S. Naval Institute Blog*, September 2012, no. 24.
[15] Sam LaGrone, "Pentagon Drops Air Sea Battle Name, Concept Lives On," *U.S. Naval Institute News*, January 20, 2015.

As the impetus for the ASB concept, long-distance capabilities have emerged to challenge the supremacy of US military forces in theaters of operation. For example, China is reported to have anti-ship capabilities (the DF-26 ASBM) that are capable of striking large- and medium-size ships at a distance of 3,000 to 4,000 kilometers away, making the DF-26 ASBM an important weapon in an A2/AD arsenal.[16] Likewise, cyber weapons can be launched from anywhere on the planet and create effects within moments. The compression of time and space in cyberspace poses a formidable challenge for counter-A2/AD strategies. Compounding the time-space compression is the fact that cyber weapons are overwhelmingly precision weapons. Precision weapons used to be very expensive and thus limited to the capabilities of only a few nation-states with advanced militaries, but cyber weapons are typically much less expensive to develop than traditional kinetic weapons and thus are available to a wider range of actors and potential adversaries. Because of this evolution in technology, precision weapons are no longer limited to line-of-sight, blue water, or over-the-horizon military capabilities; cyber weapons can be launched with a keystroke from around the globe and still deliver precise effects almost instantaneously.[17]

In January 2012, the DoD released the Joint Operational Access Concept (JOAC), which described how military forces will use cross-domain synergy to achieve operational access in the face of A2/AD threats by states and non-state actors. This seventy-five-page document is dedicated to defining a strategy for defeating A2/AD threats around the world and in all domains, including cyberspace. The goal of A2/AD is to control access to and within an operating environment. In addition, an important goal of A2/AD is to convince potential adversaries that you control access to the operating environment, in order to deter conflict and an armed contest for control of the environment. The capability to conduct A2/AD provides strategic leverage over adversaries in war and peacetime.[18]

A2/AD in cyberspace is of significant and increasing concern for US national security, as well as for the security of other nations. In the JOAC, the DoD identified three trends that directly led to the increase of A2/AD capabilities around the world in recent years. One of these trends is the *"emergence of space and cyberspace as increasingly important and contested domains"* (emphasis added) as a factor affecting the rise of A2/AD threats. In addition to proliferation of advanced technologies and changing US defensive posture, the proliferation of and dependence on cyberspace is a leading factor in the A2/AD threat.[19] Furthermore, one of the main precepts identified for

---

[16]  Richard D. Fisher Jr., "Df-26 Irbm May Have Asm Variant, China Reveals at 3 September Parade," *IHS Jane's Defence Weekly*, September 2, 2015.

[17]  Peter Dombrowski and Chris C. Demchak, "Cyber War, Cybered Conflict, and the Maritime Domain," *Naval War College Review*, 67, no. 2 (2014): 83–87.

[18]  Admiral Jonathan Greenert, "Projecting Power, Assuring Access," *The Official Blog of Chief of Naval Operations Admiral Jonathan Greenert* (2012), http://cno.navylive.dodlive.mil/2012/05/10/projecting-power-assuring-access/.

[19]  U.S. Department of Defense, "Joint Operational Access Concept," ii.

achieving operational access in the face of armed opposition is to "protect space and cyber assets while attacking the enemy's cyber and space capabilities."[20]

The counter-A2/AD operations and strategies have continued to evolve since the JOAC was released in 2012. In particular, JOAC's definition of cyberspace was superseded just a year later by the Joint Publication (JP) 3–12, Cyberspace Operations, which defined cyberspace as

> the global domain within the information environment consisting of the interde-pendent network of information technology infrastructures and resident data, including the Internet, telecommunications networks, computer systems, and embedded processors and controllers.[21]

According to JP 3–12, integration of cyberspace is necessary specifically for commanders to conduct cyberspace operations "to retain freedom of maneuver in cyberspace, accomplish the joint force commander's objectives, deny freedom of action to adversaries, and enable other operational activities."[22] Thus, while not specifically mentioning counter-A2/AD strategies, it is clear that cyberspace has an important role to play in joint-A2/AD operations.

The 2012 DoD strategic guidance, *Sustaining U.S. Global Leadership: Priorities for 21st Century Defense*, outlines the ten primary missions of the US armed forces in this century. The following two directly relate to A2/AD and cyberspace.

### Project Power Despite Anti-Access/Area Denial Challenges

In order to credibly deter potential adversaries and to prevent them from achieving their objectives, the United States must maintain its ability to project power in areas in which our access and freedom to operate are challenged. In these areas, sophis-ticated adversaries will use asymmetric capabilities, to include electronic and cyber warfare, ballistic and cruise missiles, advanced air defenses, mining, and other methods, to complicate our operational calculus. States such as China and Iran will continue to pursue asymmetric means to counter our power projection capabilities, while the proliferation of sophisticated weapons and technology will extend to non-state actors as well. Accordingly, the U.S. military will invest as required to ensure its ability to operate effectively in anti-access and area denial (A2/AD) environments. This will include implementing the Joint Operational Access Concept, sustaining our undersea capabilities, developing a new stealth bomber, improving missile defenses, and continuing efforts to enhance the resiliency and effectiveness of critical space-based capabilities.

### Operate Effectively in Cyberspace and Space

Modern armed forces cannot conduct high-tempo, effective operations without reliable information and communication networks and assured access to cyberspace

---

[20]   Ibid., iii.
[21]   U.S. Department of Defense, "Joint Publication (JP) 3–12, Cyberspace Operations," (2013), v.
[22]   Ibid., vi.

and space. Today space systems and their supporting infrastructure face a range of threats that may degrade, disrupt, or destroy assets. Accordingly, DoD will continue to work with domestic and international allies and partners and invest in advanced capabilities to defend its networks, operational capability, and resiliency in cyberspace and space.[23]

These missions are part of the overall plan to transition US defense enterprise from dealing with current security threats to preparing for and facing future challenges, with the intention of protecting a broad range of national security interests as well as rebalance and reform after protracted conflicts in Southwest Asia. The fact that A2/AD strategy and cyberspace feature so prominently in this plan is an indication that these types of challenges are being taken very seriously at the highest level of government and are receiving funding despite the recent fiscal environment of reduced defense spending.

On January 8, 2015, the joint staff at the Pentagon announced the new Joint Concept for Access and Maneuver in the Global Commons (JAM-GC), which builds off of the Air Sea Battle concept and, in terms of naming, better represents the integration and deployment of land forces to counter-A2/AD operations. As of the time of writing, it is unclear what impact this new evolution will have on counter-A2/AD strategies.

Finally, the United States must keep up with innovation – and threats – in cyberspace if it hopes to remain competitive in that domain. According to the top White House cyber security advisor Michael Daniel, the United States risks turning cyberspace into a "strategic liability" if it does not address "underlying, fundamental cybersecurity challenges."[24] In order to address these challenges, the White House released the Cyberspace National Action Plan, which is designed to bring together private and public sector experts in order to address the most significant challenges to cyber security. It also invests over $19 billion for cyber security, as part of the president's 2017 budget.[25]

## A2/AD OPERATIONS IN CYBERSPACE

With this understanding of A2/AD in other domains and the policy environment, we may wonder what A2/AD in cyberspace looks like, of what actions it consists, and whether it follows the same patterns as A2/AD in other domains, in terms of force superiority, duration, and stealth. There are two types of A2/AD in cyberspace:

---

[23]  U.S. Department of Defense, "Sustaining U.S. Global Leadership: Priorities for 21st Century Defense," (2012), 4–5.

[24]  Elias Groll, "White House: The Internet May Be a Strategic Liability to the West," *Foreign Policy*, February 11, 2016.

[25]  Office of the Press Secretary, "Factsheet: Cybersecurity National Action Plan," news release, February 9, 2016, www.whitehouse.gov/the-press-office/2016/02/09/fact-sheet-cybersecurity-national-action-plan.

strategic and tactical. Tactical A2/AD operations seek to block access to specific portions of cyberspace, such as databases, communications technology, global positioning systems, or weapons systems. Tactical A2/AD is extraordinarily important because it allows one side to prevent the other from using specific resources that are connected to cyberspace. This means that cyber actions can prevent an adversary from using precision-guided missile systems or create confusion and chaos within a navigational system, making all weapons systems connected to the navigational system unreliable. Tactical A2/AD could also mean neutralizing a particular type of cyber attack or "cyber fire." Given the interconnectedness of modern technology, especially military equipment, tactical A2/AD is a serious concern because penetration of one system could compromise a large number of advanced capabilities. The issue of tactical A2/AD is being addressed by militaries and techies the world over, and it is not the subject of this research.

This research focuses on strategic cyber A2/AD, which is access to cyberspace itself, not simply the systems and equipment that connect to it. The strategic cyber A2/AD concept flows from the premise that everything is interconnected, and, thus, the most effective way to damage an adversary is to attack its access to the network as a whole. Through strategic A2/AD operations, an adversary would not have the ability to bring any cyber-based capabilities to bear, whether they are communications technology, precision-guided missiles, or defensive maneuvering within the parts of the electromagnetic spectrum. In the twenty-first century, a new center of gravity for militaries, and likely for civil societies, may well be cyberspace. The ability to deny access to cyberspace or seriously degrade the capacity to operate in cyberspace means that forces can hold a necessary capability in jeopardy. But how can this be done? Through what means can militaries, governments, and societies be denied access to the global network of networks that is cyberspace? And what effect would this have on the rest of the world?

In addition, there is a serious question of whether or not the United States would employ strategic A2/AD operations in cyberspace, given the fact that the United States strongly supports access to information and freedom of communication and has, at times, treated cyberspace like a "global commons." Strategic A2/AD operations in cyberspace could be viewed as running counter to that policy and the long-standing tradition embodied in the right to freedom of speech. Furthermore, from diplomatic, intelligence, and operational standpoints, there are negative effects of what may essential be considered a cyber blockade. Some US citizens may be affected, resistance movements that the United States supports could be harmed, and electronic intelligence gathering efforts within the affected region may be halted. For example, in the aftermath of the 2015 Paris terrorist attacks, the cyber vigilante group Anonymous declared "full-scale cyber war" on the Islamic State and claimed to have exposed or dismantled nearly 4,000 pro-Islamic State Web sites or accounts. The move was intended to undermine Islamic State's operations and global online recruitment efforts, but it had the secondary effect of interrupting surveillance and intelligence gathering operations being conducted by the governments around the world, including in the United States.[26] These are real challenges and potential tension between a US commitment to open access in cyberspace and an offensive A2/AD strategy. While denying access is unaligned with current US policy, it is nevertheless a potential tool, and a non-kinetic weapon, in the arsenal of international relations. However at odds it may appear to be with current policy, it is still essential to evaluate the advantages and disadvantages of strategic A2/AD operations in cyberspace, even if it seems that at the moment the United States would not pursue this course of action, because future circumstances may warrant reconsideration of this policy. For example, in the event of a large-scale war with a near competitor, the United States most certainly would revisit peacetime positions of freedom of information and open access for its adversary. In the meantime, an enhanced understanding of strategic A2/AD in cyberspace from both the offensive and defensive positions will improve counter-A2/AD planning.

*Legal Considerations for Strategic A2/AD in Cyberspace*

Another question is whether or not strategic A2/AD operations in cyberspace would be considered legal. Depending upon how it is conducted, there may be inconsistencies with existing treaties or international law. The leading body of legal scholarship on international law and cyberspace, *The Tallinn Manual on the International Law Applicable to Cyber Warfare*, comes closest to addressing strategic A2/AD operations in cyberspace when it discusses blockading and cordoning off operations zones in cyberspace.[27] However, *The Tallinn Manual* ultimately concludes with a division among leading legal experts as to whether blockades and operations zones in cyberspace should carry the same legal implications as those activities in other domains.[28] On land, at sea, and in the air, blockades and operations zones require international consensus through an organization like the United Nations Security Council as peacekeeping or humanitarian operations, or else they are considered acts of war.

With regard to blockade operations in cyberspace, *The Tallinn Manual* states:[29]

> The question of whether and to what extent the law of blockade applies to in the cyber context proved to be a particularly challenging issue for the International

---

[26]   Dominique Mosbergen, "Anonymous Declares War on Isis after Paris Attacks," *Huffington Post*, November 17, 2015; "Hacker Vigilante Group Anonymous Ramps up Fight against Isis Online," *CBS News*, November 19, 2015.

[27]   According to *The Tallinn Manual*, "Operations zones include, inter alia, exclusion zones, no-fly zones, warning zones, and the immediate vicinity of naval or aerial operations. They are not 'free zones' or 'areas of unrestricted warfare.' " Michael Schmitt, ed. *The Tallinn Manual on the International Law Applicable to Cyber Warfare* (New York, NY: Cambridge University Press, 2013), 199.

[28]   Ibid., 195–202.   [29]   Ibid., 195.

Group of Experts. Blockade is a method of warfare consisting of belligerent operations to prevent all vessels and aircraft (enemy and neutral) from entering or exiting specified ports, airports, or coastal areas belonging to, occupied by, or under the control of an enemy belligerent State. A blockade may be established as part of military operations directed against military forces or as an economic operation with the strategic goal of weakening an enemy's military power through the degradation of its economy.

It goes on to evaluate how blockade operations in cyberspace compare, or could compare, with the traditional elements of maritime and aerial blockades.[30] The issues of whether or not cyber activities could amount to a blockade led to debate and dissent among the legal experts, with the minority asserting that it was merely jamming, and the majority noting that naval and aerial blockades were often enacted to achieve specific goals, such as create a negative effect on the enemy's economy. Given the importance of cyberspace to modern economic activities, the majority concluded that "it is reasonable to apply the law of blockade to operations designed to block cyber communications into and out of territory under enemy control."[31] Furthermore, the majority of experts assess that these activities are "qualitatively distinct from jamming communications."[32]

With regard to cyber zones in particular, the experts "emphasized the difficulty of defining zones in cyberspace. Moreover, compliance with the terms of a defined zone might be technically challenging since in many cases the communications concerned may rely upon cyber infrastructure over which the sender has no control."[33]

## CONCLUSION

A2/AD strategies began in ancient Greece with maritime operations designed to capitalize on geographical conditions in order to undermine the strength and numerical superiority of Xerxes' great army, but they have evolved far beyond that. A2/AD strategies can be implemented by either side, whether they are militarily superior or inferior, and the blessings of geography can play a pivotal role in determining the success or failure of an A2/AD strategy. A2/AD operations can take place on land, at sea, and in the air, and, increasingly, it appears that they are relevant for cyberspace. The most important limitation of an A2/AD strategy, though, is that it alone cannot

---

[30] The common elements of blockade are as follows: They must be declared and notified; the declaration must specify the commencement, duration, location, and extent of the blockade; it must be effective; forces maintaining the blockade must be located at a distance specified by military operations; lawful means and warfare operations may be used to enforce a blockade; access to neutral ports, airports, and coastal areas may not be blocked; the termination of the blockade must be announced and notified; and the blockade must be applied impartially to all states.

[31] Schmitt, *The Tallinn Manual on the International Law Applicable to Cyber Warfare*, 197.

[32] Ibid.   [33] Ibid., 199–200.

achieve military success. A2/AD strategies can prevent an adversary from gaining access and achieving its objective, but it cannot militarily defeat an enemy without additional military action or exogenous events, such as a lack of resources or political will (i.e., Xerxes' army was weakened by the anti-access strategy but retreated only when faced with starvation).

The US Department of Defense views A2/AD primarily as a strategy to be employed by a militarily inferior force, and, thus, US policy focuses on reducing vulnerabilities to A2/AD efforts and joint military operations that can be employed to counter A2/AD operations. While the policy has not yet addressed strategic A2/AD in cyberspace specifically, it repeatedly points to the imperative of maintaining freedom of maneuver in and reliable access to cyberspace as a foundational and critically enabling component of military actions. As the JAM-GC continues to evolve in parallel with other executive branch initiatives to increase cyber security nationwide, it is likely that the policy will evolve to directly address strategic A2/AD in cyberspace.

Strategic A2/AD in cyberspace focuses on access to cyberspace as a domain or substrate. It goes beyond jamming of discrete systems and platforms, or the crashing of a network, to address fundamental access to cyberspace – an environment on which so much else in modern society is predicated. International law is still evolving to address challenges posed by cyber warfare, but leading international experts have acknowledged that this is not only technically feasible, but consistent with other warfare operations that are governed by international law. The following chapters will address how strategic A2/AD operations may be achieved at the physical and logic layers of cyberspace

# 3

# The Physical Layer

The physical layer of cyberspace is comprised of physical elements, from fiber optic cables to cell towers, to computers and servers. Of chief importance are the fiber optic cables that traverse the globe, overland and undersea, and transmit data packages from one location to another. In addition to these cables, there are physical nodes of cables (where cables come together) called Internet exchange points, as well as server farms that centralize the processing of data packages and route them to their final destination. Additionally, satellites essential to government and commercial communications exist, although they transmit only a small fraction of the information that flows through cyberspace. Lastly, the electromagnetic (EM) spectrum is a constituent part of cyberspace – essential to its functioning and basic operations.

## CABLES

### Submarine Cables

Submarine cables traverse ocean, sea, and lake floors, carrying about 95 percent of all intercontinental telecommunications traffic in the form of voice and data. International banking and finance activities are highly dependent on these cables, as are the government and military. Data and voice communications can be passed via satellite, but it is significantly less expensive and faster to use fiber optic cables. These cables are the fibers that hug the globe and underpin the modern telecommunications system.[1]

Russell, Alison Lawlor. "Anti-Access/Area Denial @ The Physical Layer of Cyberspace." In 2015, 7th International Conference on Cyber Conflict: Architectures of Cyberspace, edited by M. Maybaum, A. M. Osula, and L. Lindstrom, 153–168. NATO CCD COE Publications, Tallinn, 2015.
[1] D. Burnett, L. Carter, S. Drew, G. Marle, L. Hagadorn, D. Bartlett-MacNeil, and N. Irvine, "Submarine Cables and the Oceans – Connecting the World," in UNEP-WCMC Biodiversity Series (ICPC/UNEP/UNEP-WCMC, 2009), 3.

There are approximately 1.197 million kilometers of undersea cables.[2] There are 291 in-service fiber optic cables around the world.[3] The longest cable systems connect continents, while shorter systems are laid along coastlines to avoid the problems of terrestrial cables and provide additional resiliency. The highest concentration of cables connects the east coast of the United States with Europe and the largest-capacity cables connect New York and the United Kingdom.[4] Figure 3.1 shows the location, routes, and end points of submarine cables around the world.

Most submarine telecommunications cables are fiber optic cables, especially newer cable systems. The older coaxial cables are still in use in some places, but their bandwidth capacity is much more limited. Fiber optic cables have become the primary cable used due to increased demand, changes in technology, and reduced cost.[5]

While these cables may be relatively new, submarine telecommunications cables are not. The first underwater cable, a copper-based telegraph cable, was laid in 1850 across the English Channel to connect the United Kingdom and France.[6] Eight years later, the first trans-Atlantic cable was laid, connecting the United States and the United Kingdom. It was a huge technological advance for the day, although the reception was terrible by modern standards, taking 2 minutes and 5 seconds to transmit a single character and more than 17 hours to transmit the first message.[7]

Likewise, tampering with underwater cables is also nothing new. As far back as the Spanish-American War, undersea telegraph cables were destroyed as part of the campaign to sever trans-Atlantic communications links.[8] During the Cold War, the United States famously tapped into Soviet cables to listen to conversations behind the Iron Curtain.[9] More recently, in 2013 three men were arrested for trying to cut through an undersea cable off the coast of Alexandria, Egypt.[10] Whether they are subjected to tampering or destruction, these cables can suffer from unintentional damage as well as sabotage, which threatens to undermine the efficiency, reliability, and security of the global network.

---

[2] Adam Blenford and Christine Jeavans, "After Snowden: How Vulnerable Is the Internet?," *BBC News*, January 27, 2014.

[3] Amy Nordrum, "Hibernia Networks Bets Speed of New Fiber Optic Cable Will Win Customers in Crowded North Atlantic Corridor," *International Business Times*, August 12, 2015.

[4] U.S. Department of Homeland Security, "Characteristics and Common Vulnerabilities Infrastructure Category: Cable Landing Stations" (Draft – Version 1, January 15, 2004), 2–3.

[5] U.S. Department of Homeland Security, "Characteristics and Common Vulnerabilities Infrastructure Category," 1.

[6] Burnett et al., "Submarine Cables and the Oceans," 3.

[7] Duncan Geere, "How the First Cable Was Laid across the Atlantic," *Wired*, January 18, 2011.

[8] Charles Cheney Hyde, *International Law, Chiefly as Interpreted and Applied by the United States*, 2nd rev. edn., 3 vols. (Boston, MA: Little, Brown and Company, 1945), 1956.

[9] Sherry Sontag, Christopher Drew, and Annette Lawrence Drew, *Blind Man's Bluff: The Untold Story of American Submarine Espionage* (New York: Public Affairs, 1998).

[10] "Egypt Arrests as Undersea Internet Cable Cut Off Alexandria," *BBC News*, March 27, 2013.

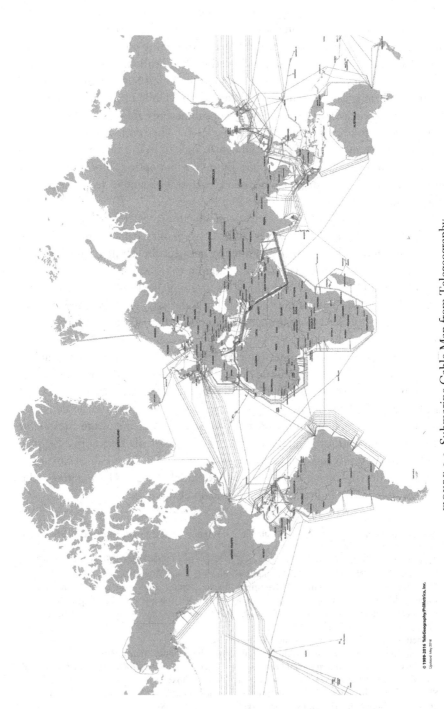

FIGURE 3.1 Submarine Cable Map from Telegeography

Source: "Submarine Cable Map," TeleGeography, www.submarinecablemap.com/. Also available at: www.iscpc.org/cable-data/.

There are approximately 100–150 cable faults or damages every year. Most of the damage that submarine cables suffer is accidental, such as ships dropping anchor in the wrong place and damaging the cables as they run through shallower waters. Fishing gear such as trawls are the most common culprit for damage to cables, accounting for roughly half of cable cuts. Over the past five decades, fishing gear and anchors combined have represented approximately 70 percent of damage done to submarine cables.[11] As a result, the location of submarine telecommunications cables and their landing stations are often marked on nautical charts and coastal maps so that ship operators and others may avoid them. These cable cuts happen frequently, but most of them are minor and result in little disruption in service.

Submarine cables may also be damaged due to natural disasters and earthquakes, which represent approximately 12 percent of damage to cables.[12] These events are relatively rare, but they can render catastrophic damage to telecommunications systems. On May 23, 2003, Algeria experienced an earthquake that damaged its telecommunications cables and its satellite ground stations, thus severing almost all of its international telecommunications services. Furthermore, the recurring aftershocks from the earthquake impeded repairs of the submarine cables, which were not completed until June 21, 2003.[13]

Finally, deliberate state action and other human action account for approximately 8 percent of cable damage.[14] Human actions may include dredging (such as that associated with beach replenishment), pipeline construction, oil and gas extraction, dumping, and scientific research. Fortunately, cuts near the shore can be repaired relatively quickly because the cables are more accessible. Damage to cables farther out at sea and at depths of more than 4,000 meters takes longer to repair and requires specialized equipment.[15]

There is no force tasked with protecting submarine cables, and the responsibility to avoid the cables falls to individual mariners, who are expected to consult the latest charts and abide by local laws to protect cables. In some places, coast guards and navies focused on littoral operations may have an increased responsibility to protect this critical infrastructure because these cables are most vulnerable as they come ashore on the beachhead, where they ultimately meet pipes that protect them as they run inland. Thus, maritime military and law enforcement forces (i.e., navies and coast guards) potentially have a role to play in monitoring and protecting critical infrastructure for cyberspace.

---

[11] Burnett et al., "Submarine Cables and the Oceans," 45.   [12] Ibid.

[13] U.S. Department of Homeland Security, "Characteristics and Common Vulnerabilities Infrastructure Category," 7–8.

[14] Burnett et al., "Submarine Cables and the Oceans," 45.   [15] Ibid., 44–47.

### Terrestrial Cables

Cable networks that run over land consist of physical lines, transmission line amplifiers, network protection equipment, wavelength termination equipment, and supervisory circuitry.[16] Submarine cables come ashore at cable landing stations, where they are then connected to communications networks on land. Some of these stations are located in densely populated areas, such as New York City, while others are in more remote locations, such as Nedonna Beach, Oregon. At the landing stations, the cables (or fibers, as they are sometimes called) are encased in protective tubes or casings and trenched (i.e., placed in a trench dug for this purpose) or routed along existing rights of way, such as railroad tracks and bridges. Cables, protected by these tubes, bring connectivity inland.[17]

Terrestrial cables are most exposed at the cable landing sites, where they are vulnerable and can be subject to accidental or intentional damage. Common threats to cables include attacks that target the fiber itself, the switching/network control equipment to which it attaches, and the electrical power system that supports it. The cables that are exposed above ground (for instance, from the shoreline to a building or along a right of way) and those that are subterraneous but easily accessible (i.e., below a manhole cover) are most vulnerable to damage.[18]

Cable landing sites often consist of one building with telecommunications equipment. Localized damage to cables and equipment at landing stations is relatively easy to repair, unless the area is unreachable due to debris, flooding, contamination, or other conditions that may be created by an attack or a natural disaster. The primary security of the cables lies in the resiliency and flexibility of the network. First, the network has "self-healing" powers to reroute traffic away from nodes or pathways. Thus, damage to one cable or landing station is unlikely to have a noticeable effect on routine operations. Second, the cables, landing stations, and other stations are not permanently tied to specific locations and can be relocated to another place that is more secure.[19] Cyberspace is a man-made network; thus, we have the ability to change elements of its geographical configuration.

Damage to the landing stations themselves can be conducted directly through a physical attack on the building (such as a bombing or armed assault), indirectly (such as an attack on the power supply), or through internal sabotage (such as a computer virus or worm, fire, or physical damage). Indirect attacks on power sources are unlikely to be successful because landing stations have battery backup power generator systems, but they are still possible. More likely, a disruption of

---

[16] U.S. Department of Homeland Security, "Characteristics and Common Vulnerabilities Infrastructure Category," 6.

[17] Ibid., 4–6; Andrew Blum, *Tubes : A Journey to the Center of the Internet*, 1st edn. (New York: Ecco, 2012).

[18] U.S. Department of Homeland Security, "Characteristics and Common Vulnerabilities Infrastructure Category," 7.

[19] Ibid., 6–7.

power to a cable landing station would be part of a larger interruption of service (attack or otherwise) on the regional area.[20] There are typically minimal forms of physical protection for cable landing sites, making a physical attack possible. Many cable landing sites are completely unprotected, simply small buildings on a beach somewhere. Of those that have some protection, they typically have chain-link fences and basic video surveillance equipment. Thus, as these sites are usually small areas with limited physical barriers, it is relatively easy to conduct physical damage to this type of infrastructure.

Another challenge to managing the vulnerabilities of the physical infrastructure is that the information about the location of cables landing ashore is publicly knowable in many places. In the United States, the Federal Communications Commission (FCC) mandates the public availability of locations for all cables that touch its shores.[21] Furthermore, there are numerous articles discussing risk to critical infrastructure, including cyber infrastructure, that provide specific information about the location of some of the infrastructure.[22] In addition, it is not difficult to obtain the equipment to find a cable line underground and destroy it – a line tracer and an axe will suffice. Despite this, the interconnectedness of land networks provides resiliency for the system.[23]

## SATELLITES

Satellites are another essential part of cyberspace, although they transmit only 5 percent of voice and data telecommunications. When compared with fiber optic cable networks, they are five times slower and have 0.3 percent of the capacity. They are also more than fifty times more expensive per megabits per second. Furthermore, the design lifespan of satellites is ten to fifteen years, whereas cables can last twenty-five years.[24] Table 3.1 compares satellite and submarine cable operations.

Private sector communications satellites provide an array of service, including voice and Internet service. These satellites usually orbit in medium Earth orbit, a distance of 200–930 miles from Earth. The larger the satellite, the greater the power capacity, and thus the higher an orbit it is capable of achieving. The major players in private sector communications satellites are ViaSat, Space Systems/Loral, O3b, Eutelsat, and IntelSat.[25]

---

[20] Ibid., 7.
[21] Sam Biddle, "How to Destroy the Internet," Gizmodo.com, http://gizmodo.com/5912383/how-to-destroy-the-internet.
[22] Paul Saffo, "Disrupting Undersea Cables: Cyberspace's Hidden Vulnerability," International Relations and Security Network (ISN), www.isn.ethz.ch/Digital-Library/Articles/Detail/?id=162869.
[23] www.bbc.co.uk/news/technology-25832341, Blenford and Jeavans, "After Snowden"
[24] John K. Crain, *Assessing Resilience in the Global Undersea Cable Infrastructure* (Monterey, CA: Naval Postgraduate School, 2012), 3.
[25] Alistair Barr and Andy Pasztor, "Google Invests in Satellites to Spread Internet Access," *The Wall Street Journal*, June 1, 2014.

TABLE 3.1 *Comparison of Satellites and Submarine Fiber Optic Cables across Several Key Factors in Telecommunications*

| Comparison Factor | Satellite | Optical Subsea |
| --- | --- | --- |
| Latency | 250 milliseconds | 50 milliseconds |
| Design life | 10–15 years | 25 years |
| Capacity | 48,000 channels | 160,000,000 channels |
| Unit cost per Mbps capacity | US$737,316 | US$14,327 |
| Share to traffic: 1995 | 50 percent | 50 percent |
| Share to traffic: 2008 | 3 percent | 97 percent |

*Source:* John K. Crain, "Assessing Resilience in the Global Undersea Cable Infrastructure" (Naval Postgraduate School, 2012), 3, Adapted from C. Donovan, "Twenty Thousand Leagues under the Sea: A Life Cycle Assessment of Fibre Optic Submarine Cable Systems" Master's Thesis, The Royal Institute of Technology, Stockholm, Sweden, 2009.

Satellite access faces several challenges for end users, in particular: high cost, signal latency, signal strength, and interference. With regard to the economics of satellites, they have high upfront costs ($50 to $400 million for a large satellite)[26] and marginal returns, particularly communications and Internet satellites that are competing with the more efficient cables that have much faster rates of transmission.[27] Signal strength and integrity are also an issue; due to interference and power requirements for satellites, signal reliability can be unstable.

Additionally, hardware capability is particularly important for satellites. Satellite manufacturing is a time-consuming process and requires significant lead time, such as five to ten years for larger satellites. Following Moore's law,[28] rapid improvement in technological capabilities means that by the time satellites are launched, their hardware may already be out of date. Microsatellites, which can be developed in one to two years at a cost of only a few million dollars, may be a solution to this problem.[29]

Satellites face vulnerabilities in space and on the ground. In space, their primary challenges include missiles, space debris, and hacking. On the ground, their control stations are physical targets that can be compromised by deliberate action, accidental causes, or acts of nature.

Antisatellite missile systems have been a threat since the 1950s and continue to be developed today. In 2007, China demonstrated its antisatellite missile capability by

[26] "The Cost of Building and Launching a Satellite," www.globalcomsatphone.com/hughesnet/satellite/costs.html.

[27] Latency is the measure of response time, but the speed of a network commonly refers to throughput/bandwidth.

[28] Generally speaking, Moore's law is the prediction that processing powers for computers will double every two years.

[29] Conrad de Aenlle, "U.K. Firm Finds Niche in 'Discount' Satellites," *The New York Times*, June 19, 2001

destroying a defunct weather satellite at 537 miles above Earth. Similarly, the United States destroyed a spy satellite in 2008 at 150 miles above Earth.

Space debris is also a threat to satellites. Debris is created by man-made objects in space, including old satellites, spent rocket stages, and fragments from erosion, collision, and disintegration of items in orbit. In 2009, the US Iridium 33 communications satellite collided with a defunct Russian military communications satellite, Cosmos 2251. The collision caused a significant increase in debris, requiring the International Space Station to execute avoidance maneuvers.[30] Likewise, the aforementioned Chinese weather satellite that was destroyed in 2007 resulted in significant debris due to the way in which it was shot down.[31]

Satellite hacking has already been reported.[32] Given that satellites are often sent up with outdated technology, vulnerabilities are likely to grow over time. The technological expertise required to hack a satellite may be found within state resources and armed forces, as well as within the hacking community. Indeed, China was accused of hacking into US weather satellites in 2014,[33] and there are also claims of black hat and white hat hackers hacking satellites.[34]

Satellite communications rely on ground stations to receive information and track satellites moving through orbit. The ground stations function as a hub to receive information from the satellite and connect it with terrestrial communication networks, such as the Internet. Ground stations can also be used to upload computer programs or issue commands to the satellite. These stations are susceptible to physical attack as well as natural events, such as earthquakes, tornadoes, and tsunamis.

## ELECTROMAGNETIC SPECTRUM

Despite being invisible to the naked human eye, the EM spectrum is a physical entity that underpins the operations of cyberspace. This spectrum is, in fact, a constituent element of cyberspace and critical for all activities in cyberspace.[35]

The EM spectrum consists of a range of all possible frequencies of EM radiation within the environment. This EM radiation travels in waves and allows humans to understand the environment around them through sight and sound. Light and

---

[30] "International Space Station Again Dodges Debris," *Orbital Debris Quarterly News, National Aeronautics and Space Administration*, 15, no. 3 (July 2011).

[31] "Chinese Asat Test," Center for Space Standards & Innovation, www.centerforspace.com/asat/.

[32] Mary Pat Flaherty, Jason Samenow, and Lisa Rein, "Chinese Hack U.S. Weather Systems, Satellite Network," *Washington Post*, November 12, 2014.

[33] Ibid.

[34] Stephen Northcutt, "Are Satellites Vulnerable to Hackers?" www.sans.edu/research/security-laboratory/article/satellite-dos.

[35] The electromagnetic spectrum is the range of all types of EM radiation, which is the energy that travels and spreads as it goes out.

colors perceptible to the human eye are found within one small sliver of the EM spectrum, while the rest of the spectrum is invisible to the naked eye. The spectrum ranges from low-frequency waves, such as radio waves, at one end, to high-frequency waves, such as X-rays and gamma rays, at the other end.

The portion of the EM spectrum that is most relevant to cyberspace is that which has longer wavelengths and lower frequency: radio waves and microwaves. This subsection of the spectrum ranges in frequency from $10^{11}$ to $10^5$ waves per second, or roughly 600 kHz to 100 GHz. Radio and microwaves are the avenue for the transmission of data and information via radar (on which satellites depend), wireless Internet, over-the-air television broadcasts, mobile phones, and AM and FM radio. Without this portion of the naturally occurring EM spectrum, there would be no wireless, mobile, or satellite communication.

CYBER DEPENDENCY ON AND RELATION TO THE EM SPECTRUM

Cyberspace and the EM spectrum are two separate but interrelated spheres. Cyberspace is dependent upon the EM spectrum, but cannot be merged or joined with it since there are parts of the EM spectrum that extend well beyond the realm of cyberspace. Some of the capabilities and vulnerabilities within the EM spectrum also apply to cyberspace, since there is some overlap between the two realms. In essence, cyberspace is the man-made infrastructure that operates in the naturally occurring, physical arena known as the EM spectrum.[36] Figure 3.2 depicts the DoD's graphical understanding of the intersection of cyberspace operations, electronic warfare, and management operations within the EM spectrum.

For decades, military forces have operated in the EM spectrum and employed electronic warfare (EW) tactics in support of military operations. Given that cyberspace constitutes a large portion of the information environment and the EM spectrum is a constituent element of cyberspace, EW is a part of cyberspace. The purpose of EW is "to deny an opponent an advantage in the EM spectrum and ensure friendly and unimpeded access to the EM portion of the information environment."[37] EW uses offensive and defensive tactics to insure unimpeded access to the EM spectrum through detection, denial, deception, disruption, degradation, protection, and destruction.[38] Traditional EW activities include jamming and spoofing radars and communication links.[39] The underlying physics of

---

[36]  Paraphrasing Rear Admiral Filipowski, former director for Electronic and Cyber Warfare in the Office of the Chief of Naval Operations, as quoted in Mickey Batson and Matthew Labert, "Expanding the Non-Kinetic Warfare Arsenal," *U.S. Naval Institute Proceedings*, 138, no. 1 (2012).

[37]  U.S. Department of Defense, "Joint Publication 3–13.1 Electronic Warfare," ed. U.S. Department of Defense (January 25, 2007), v. Available at: http://fas.org/irp/doddir/dod/jp3-13-1.pdf.

[38]  Ibid., v–vi.

[39]  "Ea-6b Prowler," U.S. Naval Air Systems Command, www.navair.navy.mil/index.cfm?fuseaction= home.display&key=C8B54023-C006-4699-BD20-9A45FBA02B9A.

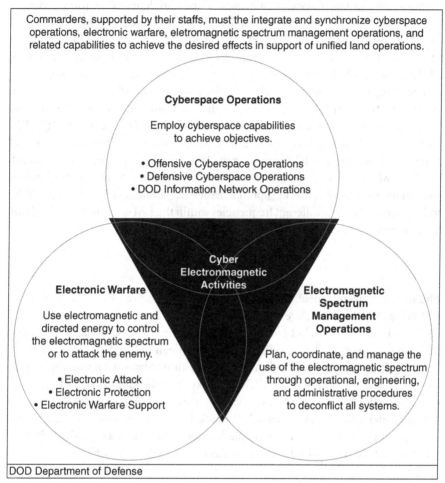

Commarders, supported by their staffs, must the integrate and synchronize cyberspace operations, electronic warfare, eletromagnetic spectrum management operations, and related capabilities to achieve the desired effects in support of unified land operations.

**Cyberspace Operations**

Employ cyberspace capabilities to achieve objectives.

• Offensive Cyberspace Operations
• Defensive Cyberspace Operations
• DOD Information Network Operations

**Cyber Electronmagnetic Activities**

**Electronic Warfare**

Use electromagnetic and directed energy to control the electromagnetic spectrum or to attack the enemy.

• Electronic Attack
• Electronic Protection
• Electronic Warfare Support

**Electromagnetic Spectrum Management Operations**

Plan, coordinate, and manage the use of the electromagnetic spectrum through operational, engineering, and administrative procedures to deconflict all systems.

DOD Department of Defense

FIGURE 3.2 Intersection of Cyberspace Operations, Electronic Warfare, and EM Spectrum Management Operations
Source: "Fm 3–38 Cyber Electromagnetic Activities" (Washington, DC: Headquarters, Department of the Army, February 2014).

offensive cyber operations and electronic attacks points to a clear overlap in the capabilities needed for each.[40]

Trends indicate that security threats involving cyberspace and the EMS will continue to evolve and grow more sophisticated. Of the likely necessary future capabilities that overlap, the two domains are spectrum warfare and agility within the EM spectrum, which will require computer systems to be more dynamic in guiding fixed-frequency communications and radar systems. Directed energy

[40] Harold T. Cole, "Warfare in the Electromagnetic Spectrum and Cyberspace: United States Air Force Cyber/Electromagnetic Warfare Command Construct" (Air War College, Air University, 2014).

weapons, such as lasers, have already been tested and deployed by the US Navy.[41] The US Air Force is also actively exploring directed energy technologies, most notably a cruise missile, called CHAMP,[42] capable of emitting an EM pulse against a target to electronically destroy its unprotected electronics. Future development of CHAMP may include directed energy weapons or cyber weapons payloads.[43]

According to US Chief of Naval Operations Admiral Jonathan Greenert in 2011, "In the next two decades, the [electromagnetic] environment may become our most critical warfighting arena. Control of information – much of it through the EM spectrum – is already growing more important than control of territory in modern warfare."[44] EW, and now EM maneuver warfare, focuses on managing and controlling the EM spectrum. Capabilities within the EM spectrum are of critical importance to the mission of achieving optimal battlespace awareness. Flexible operations and maneuverability to different frequencies within the EM spectrum allow military forces to ensure access and operations within the EW environment.[45]

### EMP Threat

The most significant threat to the EM spectrum comes from the generation of an EM pulse (EMP). The dangers of EMP attacks for electronic systems were spelled out as early as the 1960s, but continue to capture the attention of national security decision makers, as well as novelists and the American public.[46]

Many offices and agencies within the US government have been investigating the likelihood and potential impact of EMP attacks since the Cold War, and they have revitalized efforts in the post-9/11 era with the concern over rogue states or terrorist networks attempting to launch an EMP attack. In 2008, Congress received a report, at its request, on the threat to the United States of EMP attacks, particularly their effect on critical national infrastructure. According to the report,[47]

---

[41]   The USS *Ponce* was the test bed for the Navy's laser weapons system in 2013. The ship, along with its laser weapons system, was deployed to the Persian Gulf in 2014.

[42]   This cruise missile is known by the acronym CHAMP, which stands for Counter Electronics High Powered Microwave Advanced Missile Project.

[43]   Cole, "Warfare in the Electromagnetic Spectrum and Cyberspace," 13–14.

[44]   Chief of Naval Operations ADM Jonathan Greenert, October 10, 2011, quoted in "Networks and EMS (NES) Roadmap – Navy EW and Cyber Convergence," in 2011 *DoD Spectrum Workshop* (December 16, 2011).

[45]   "Electromagnetic Spectrum Maneuver Warfare," Navy Live, http://navylive.dodlive.mil/2013/10/30/ electromagnetic-spectrum-maneuver-warfare.

[46]   The third edition of *The Effects of Nuclear Weapons* was published in 1977 and included a discussion on the effects of EMPs on computer systems. In 2009, *One Second After*, a novel by William R. Forstchen about the apocalyptical life in the United States after an EMP, became a *New York Times* best seller.

[47]   Commission to Assess the Threat to the United States from Electromagnetic Pulse (EMP) Attack., *Report of the Commission to Assess the Threat to the United States from Electromagnetic Pulse (EMP) Attack: Critical National Infrastructures* (Washington, DC: Commission to Assess the Threat to the

the electromagnetic pulse generated by a high altitude nuclear explosion is one of a small number of threats that can hold our society at risk of catastrophic consequences. The increasingly pervasive use of electronics of all forms represents the greatest source of vulnerability to attack by EMP ... Because of the ubiquitous dependence of U.S. society on the electrical power system, its vulnerability to an EMP attack, coupled with the EMP's particular damage mechanisms, creates the possibility of long-term, catastrophic consequences. The implicit invitation to take advantage of this vulnerability, when coupled with increasing proliferation of nuclear weapons and their delivery systems, is a serious concern. A single EMP attack may seriously degrade or shut down a large part of the electric power grid in the geographic area of EMP exposure effectively instantaneously ... Damage to or loss of these components could leave significant parts of the electrical infrastructure out of service for periods measured in months to a year or more ... Electrical power is necessary to support other critical infrastructures, including supply and distribution of water, food, fuel, communications, transport, financial transactions, emergency services, government services, and all other infrastructures supporting the national economy and welfare. Should significant parts of the electrical power infrastructure be lost for any substantial period of time, the Commission believes that the consequences are likely to be catastrophic, and many people may ultimately die for lack of the basic elements necessary to sustain life in dense urban and suburban communities. In fact, the Commission is deeply concerned that such impacts are likely in the event of an EMP attack unless practical steps are taken to provide protection for critical elements of the electric system and for rapid restoration of electric power, particularly to essential services.

Despite the dire warnings and assessments that cover electric power, telecommunications, banking and finance sectors, petroleum and natural gas, transportation infrastructure, food and water infrastructures, emergency services, space systems, and government, it is unclear what, if anything, has been done to reduce vulnerabilities and mitigate the potential short- and long-term effects of an EMP attack. To raise the level of awareness within society of the potential for a catastrophic EMP attack on the United States, there have been several popular books published on the topic recently. Books such as *The New York Times* best seller *One Second After*[48] by William R. Forstchen and *A Nation Forsaken*[49] by F. Michael Maloof have brought to the public attention the threat of EMP attacks and the doomsday scenarios that could follow.

An EMP attack occurs when conventional explosives are detonated at high altitudes and create EM signals that interfere with the normal EM field. Nuclear explosions do the same, but in a much more significant way. The intensity, duration,

United States from Electromagnetic Pulse (EMP) Attack: For sale by the Supt. of Docs., U.S. G.P.O., 2008), vi–vii.

[48] William R. Forstchen, *One Second After*, 1st edn. (New York: Forge, 2009).

[49] F. Michael Maloof, *A Nation Forsaken: EMP, the Escalating Threat of an American Catastrophe*, 1st edn. (Washington D.C. New York: WND Books; Midpoint Trade Books (distributor), 2013).

and area that is affected by an EMP vary depending upon where the EMP device is detonated. The strongest electric fields are near the bust, typically near the Earth's surface, when the explosive is detonated. The EM waves travel in all directions, including downward and outward to the Earth and potentially beyond the horizon, for a high-yield explosion.[50]

If a nuclear explosion occurred at a higher altitude, the EM fields of a broader swath of Earth would be affected. The incendiary damage of a high-altitude blast would be much less (or none at all), but the EM damage would be far worse. If the explosion occurred 50 miles above the Earth's surface, then the affected area on the ground would have a radius of approximately 600 miles. For an explosion 100 miles in the air, the ground radius of the affected area would be approximately 900 miles. An explosion at an altitude of 200 miles, located over the center of the United States, would affect almost the entire country, as well as parts of Canada and Mexico.[51]

The electric grid, computers, and other equipment with solid-state components are particularly sensitive to an EMP.[52] Given the interconnectedness of electrical and computer systems and the modern reliance on them for all aspects of life, the consequences of an EMP could be disastrous. Satellite and ballistic missile systems would also be affected as they would be exposed directly to radiation from a high-altitude nuclear explosion.[53] An EMP attack would surge energy across the EM spectrum at a broad spectrum of frequencies. Electronic systems would be functionally damaged resulting in permanent failure, or operationally degraded leading to an inability to execute the range of functions for a period of time, which can range from days to weeks or months, or even years. The threat to the individual system is largely a function of how efficiently it collects energy from the EM spectrum, and since the more efficient systems collect more energy, they would feel the effects of an EMP attack in a larger way than would a less efficient system. Ironically, the most sophisticated and sensitive systems would be damaged the most, while the older systems and technology would likely fare much better.[54]

It is possible to protect electronic equipment from EMP attacks through shielding or hardening of the equipment. A shield composed of a continuous metal, such as steel, copper, or soft iron, if entirely surrounding the system, can protect it from EMP attacks. Vacuum tube technology is not susceptible to EMP attacks, although it is not commonly found in today's electronic systems. Finally, older studies suggest that certain types of circuit layout could reduce the vulnerability of systems, but it is unclear whether that would still hold true with today's sensitive electronics.[55]

---

[50] Samuel Glasstone and Philip J. Dolan, *The Effects of Nuclear Weapons*, 3rd edn. (Washington, DC: United States Department of Defense and the Energy Research and Development Administration, 1977), 514–519.
[51] Ibid., 519.  [52] Ibid., 521.  [53] Ibid., 522.  [54] Ibid., 524.  [55] Ibid., 526.

CONCLUSION

There are many physical attributes of cyberspace that could be manipulated in order to cut off an adversary's access to cyberspace. While fiber optic cables, particularly the submarine cables, form the backbone of the global network, there are enough redundancies built into place for most countries that it would require a coordinated effort to destroy or degrade them all simultaneously. Satellites provide additional connectivity and are essential for highly sensitive data and access in remote locations, including for forward-deployed troops, but they are limited in their bandwidth and can also be physically destroyed or manipulated. EMP attacks provide the most comprehensive method of destroying access to cyberspace, but in the process, these attacks would also destroy nearly all modern electronic systems, which could result in a humanitarian disaster and a catastrophic breakdown of all elements of society, most notably medical care, water resources, food supply, and transportation. Fortunately, there are international agreements in place that prohibit EMP attacks.[56]

---

[56] International agreements on the use of nuclear weapons and EMP attacks are discussed in Chapter 5.

# 4

# The Logic Layer

The logic layer is the central nervous system of cyberspace. It is responsible for routing data packages to their final destinations, primarily via domain name systems (DNS), Internet protocols, browsers, Web sites, and software, all of which rely on the aforementioned fiber optic cables and physical foundations. Targeted cyber attacks can manipulate the logic layer of cyberspace in a number of ways to cause it to malfunction or shut down completely in order to inhibit the flow of data.

The logic layer of cyberspace can be attacked and altered in a variety of ways through cyber attacks. Many of the central elements of the logic layer are under attack every day as malicious actors attempt to break the system. And unlike a physical attack on infrastructure, which would require time, coordination, and access in order to damage enough elements to successfully cut a state off from cyberspace, well-designed cyber attacks at the logic layer can be designed to hit multiple key nodes at once. Thus, while technologically it is much more difficult to attack the key nodes of the logic layer, there is a synergy present that could make a single, advanced cyber attack more successful at creating an A2/AD environment than many coordinated attacks on the physical infrastructure.

There are some safeguards in place to diminish the risk of cyber attacks that target these systems, including redundancies and the ability to reroute traffic through an uncompromised server. For example, when all thirteen of the Internet root servers were attacked simultaneously in 2002, several servers were able to withstand the attack and continued to operate, thus keeping the Internet functioning despite the fact that several servers were temporarily shut down by the attack.[1] Despite this attack over a decade ago, vulnerabilities still exist and can be exploited. Chief among them are the operating systems that manage the wavelengths of the fiber optic cables as they come ashore at landing sites. Using these systems, hackers can manipulate the wavelengths to alter or remove some or all of the data traffic on that cable, potentially without the operator's knowledge.[2]

---

[1] "Internet Backbone Withstands Major Attack."    [2] Sechrist, "New Threats, Old Technology," 12.

Attacks at the logic layer may take many forms. This chapter will examine the different places or nodes within the logic layer that would be the most logical targets for strategic A2/AD attacks, including root servers, Internet service providers (ISPs), and border gateways. Next, it will review in detail one particular type of attack that experts warn can "break the Internet" – distributed denial of service (DDoS) – in order to understand its potential consequences at the logic layer of cyberspace.

## ROOT SERVERS

Root servers form the most basic, core level of the Internet. These servers exist at the root of the DNS hierarchy, which converts human-readable Internet names (such as netnod.se) into numeric addresses (such as 192.71.80.109 or 2a01:3f0:1:3::109).[3] DNS is organized into a hierarchy in which each level resolves a different piece of information in the Internet name and pushes it down to that level for further resolution until finally the correct numeric webpage is identified. The root zone (where the root servers are located) is the top-level domain. The root zone deals with what comes after the "dot" in a web address – for example, where .com, .net, .org, . edu, and .gov are distinguished from each other and from all the other "dot some-things" like country codes (.us for the United States, .se for Sweden, or .no for Norway). In layman's terms, the "dot something" part of the web address is the root zone, where Internet systems begin sorting and decoding delivery addresses. It is the Internet equivalent of the postal system sorting letters based first on the country listed as the address destination, before proceeding to the next levels of information, such as state or region, city or town, street, and number.

The root zone comes from the Internet Assigned Numbers Authority (IANA) and the Internet Corporation for Names and Numbers (ICANN), two of the highest-level governing bodies of the Internet. These governing bodies ensure authenticity of the root servers and guidance for the root zones so that root servers know where to direct traffic as a matter of authenticity and reliability. Root servers publish root zones and have no authority to change them, and this authority lies exclusively with IANA and ICANN.[4]

There are thirteen root servers operated by twelve independent organizations, most of which have been in operation since the earliest days of the Internet. Many are based in the United States, reflecting the origins of the Internet as a US-based research and military network.[5] The root servers are labeled letters A through M, and their hostnames follow the pattern of a.root-server.net, b.root-server.net, and so on. Table 4.1 shows the hostname for each root server, its Internet protocol (IP) address, and the operators of that root server.[6]

---

[3] "What Are Root Name Servers?," Netnod, www.netnod.se/what-are-root-name-servers.   [4] Ibid.
[5] Ibid.   [6] "Root Servers Technical Operations Assn.," www.root-servers.org/.

TABLE 4.1 *Root Server Names, IP Addresses, and Operators*

| Hostname | IP Addresses | Operators |
|---|---|---|
| a.root-servers.net | 198.41.0.4, 2001:503:ba3e::2:30 | Verisign, Inc. |
| b.root-servers.net | 192.228.79.201, 2001:500:84::b | University of Southern California, Information Sciences Institute |
| c.root-servers.net | 192.33.4.12, 2001:500:2::c | Cogent Communications |
| d.root-servers.net | 199.7.91.13, 2001:500:2d::d | University of Maryland |
| e.root-servers.net | 192.203.230.10 | NASA Ames Research Center |
| f.root-servers.net | 192.5.5.241, 2001:500:2f::f | Internet Systems Consortium, Inc. |
| g.root-servers.net | 192.112.36.4 | US Department of Defense Network Information Center |
| h.root-servers.net | 198.97.190.53, 2001:500:1::53 | US Army Research Lab |
| i.root-servers.net | 192.36.148.17, 2001:7fe::53 | Netnod |
| j.root-servers.net | 192.58.128.30, 2001:503:c27::2:30 | Verisign, Inc. |
| k.root-servers.net | 193.0.14.129, 2001:7fd::1 | RIPE NCC |
| l.root-servers.net | 199.7.83.42, 2001:500:3::42 | ICANN |
| m.root-servers.net | 202.12.27.33, 2001:dc3::35 | WIDE Project |

Abbreviations: ICANN = Internet Corporation for Names and Numbers; IP = Internet protocol; RIPE NCC = Réseaux IP Européens Network Coordination Centre; US = United States; WIDE = Widely Integrated Distributed Environment
*Source:* Figure adapted from "Root Servers," Internet Assigned Numbers Authority (IANA), www.iana.org /domains/root/servers; "Root Servers Technical Operations Assn."

Originally, these thirteen root name servers were the only servers, and each was linked to only one IP address. However, in the early 2000s, after the 2002 attack on these servers, an effort was undertaken to expand the footprint of root servers. Today's Internet has more than 300 root servers dispersed over six continents, yet they are still reachable only by the thirteen IP addresses. The geographic dispersion of root servers means that users on any continent can reach the root servers faster and receive faster responses from local servers.[7]

Each of the twelve organizations listed above is responsible for the root server IP address that it operates. Each organization has responsibility for only one root server IP address, except for Verisign, which has two. The organizations determine from how many locations their IP address will be served; one organization only has one location, another has over one hundred locations, but altogether they number over 300 root servers. The operating organizations decide which hardware and software will be installed at their root server and how the server will be maintained, and they are responsible for funding the root server's operation.[8]

[7] "What Are Root Name Servers?"  [8] Ibid.

Root servers are critical infrastructure, but their tolerance for disturbance is high. The failure of any individual root server would likely go unnoticed by most Internet users, as other root servers would quickly pick up and answer the queries. According to Netnod, one of the twelve organizations responsible for root servers,

> if all instances of a single address are unreachable, either in general or for a specific part of the world, there are twelve more root server IP addresses to choose from. The chances of all 300-plus root servers or all thirteen root server IP addresses being unreachable at once are very small, and the root server system is, thus, very reliable.[9]

The resiliency and geographically distributed locations of the root servers were, in part, a consequence of earlier attacks to the root servers. There have been two major attacks on root servers, but neither resulted in sustained damage. There have also been technical glitches and threatened attacks but, again, nothing that resulted in sustained degradation of the system.[10]

In October 2002, an attack on the root servers caused minimal damage. The servers were not globally distributed in the way that they are dispersed today, and the fact that they were attacked at all was significant. During the attack, attackers used a botnet in an attempt to overwhelm all thirteen root servers. Many of the root servers were protected by packet filters, which redirected ping messages sent to the servers. As a result, these protected servers were able to continue to function as normal. In addition, many local DNS servers cached the IP addresses of top-level domain servers, which allowed the query process to skip the root servers altogether, thereby reducing traffic to them.[11] While some of the root servers were rendered unreachable during this attack, many others were continuously accessible during the entire duration of the attack because of their infrastructure at the network level through a combination of means such as multiple locations, excess bandwidth, hardware switch load balancing, and high path splay.[12]

On February 6, 2007, a similar type of attack occurred against root name servers. Attackers tried to overwhelm the servers with an extraordinarily high number of data packets. One of the root servers most noticeably affected was the L Root Server, operated by ICANN. In its report after the attack, ICANN said that although six of the thirteen root servers were affected, only two were seriously affected. These two

---

[9]  Ibid.
[10]  These attacks took place on October 21, 2002, and February 6, 2007; the threat came on February 12, 2012. All of these incidents will be covered in more detail later. Robert Lemos, "Assault on Net Servers Fails," published October 22, 2002, updated October 23, 2002, accessed July 1, 2015, www.cnet.com /news/assault-on-net-servers-fails/.
[11]  James F. Kurose and Keith W. Ross, *Computer Networking: A Top Down Approach*, 6th edn. (Boston: Pearson, 2013), 143.
[12]  Paul Vixie, Gerry Sneeringer, and Mark Schliefer, "Events of 21-Oct-2002," (November 24, 2002).

servers did not use Anycast technology, which was developed in the aftermath of the 2002 attacks in order to improve stability. The technology allows a number of servers in different locations to act as if they are in the same location. As a result, although there are only thirteen locations on the networks for root servers, there are hundreds of servers in different locations that can deal with requests to the thirteen root servers. The Anycast system has two advantages: First, in the event of an attack, its load can be spread out over all of the 300-plus servers instead of concentrating on thirteen; and, second, the geographic dispersion means that if something happens physically in one location, such as an earthquake, there is sufficient redundancy for the root server to remain operational.[13]

To manage the 2007 attack, engineers added more bandwidth to cope with the increased flow of packets and simultaneously tried to find patterns in the queries being sent to the root servers in order to try to filter out nefarious traffic. In this particular attack, the malicious packets were five times the size of normal packets, so engineers were able to filter them out based on size and reduce 99.7 percent of all the traffic in the system, while having virtually no impact on normal users. The report concluded that the attack originated in the Asia Pacific region but did not determine which country. Regardless, because of the practice of faking Internet addresses (called spoofing), it is entirely possible that the perpetrators of the attack were not in that region at all and triggered it from somewhere else in the world.[14]

A month after the attack, the Security and Stability Advisory Committee (SSAC) made several recommendations on how to prevent similar attacks in the future. They are as follows:

1. Those running networks should adopt "source IP address verification" – that is, improve and tighten existing systems.
2. Root server operators – and those running country code top-level domains – draw up their countermeasure policies, respond quickly to queries, and act quickly to add servers back into the system if the owner shows they have improved their security.
3. ISPs should accept DNS queries only from trusted sources (i.e., their own customers) rather than allowing anyone to use their servers.[15]

The historical precedent demonstrates that root servers are vulnerable to flooding by botnets, but due to the presence of infrastructure technology, such as Anycast, even serious attacks have thus far been negligible in their impact. The organizations in charge of operating the root servers are in frequent communications with each other and have systems and processes in place in order to manage a major attack. Security measures are still not perfect, but the act of attacking the root servers is sufficiently technically challenging that it has not yet been done successfully.

[13] "Icann Factsheet: Root Server Attack on 6 February 2007" (2007), 3.   [14] Ibid.   [15] Ibid., 5.

## BORDER GATEWAY PROTOCOLS

Border gateway protocols (BGPs) are standard routing protocols used to exchange information about routing between autonomous systems. The BGP is the protocol used by ISPs and other autonomous systems when they interact with each other to route traffic in order to provide a service, such as delivering email or displaying a webpage. BGPs determine the best route to a destination when there are multiple paths available. There are two types of BGPs: external and internal. External BGPs, or eBGPs, are those that propagate routes between ISPs, as described earlier. Internal BGPs, or iBGPs, can be used within an autonomous system in order to transmit routes that have been acquired from other autonomous systems. The eBGPs are the more significant of the two because they can adversely affect a large portion of the Internet.[16]

There are four basic components of the BGP system: speakers, peers, links, and border routers. The BGP speaker is the host that executes the protocol. BGP peers are the two different speakers (or autonomous systems) that form a connection and engage in the protocol dialogue. Links are the connections that are established between BGP peers using a reliable protocol, such as Transmission Control Protocol (TCP). Links can be external or internal, depending upon the relationship of the peers/autonomous systems. Finally, a border router is one outside of an organization's firewalls that interfaces to a physical network that is shared with border routers in other autonomous systems. It performs basic checks on network activity, including filtering of potentially harmful traffic.[17]

The BGP's architecture was built in the 1970s and founded on the assumption of trustworthiness of the networks and actors in cyberspace. It is possible, however, to exploit this trust and the system's natural architecture in order to launch an attack. It does not require new vulnerabilities, protocol errors, or software problems, just simply the existing BGP architecture.[18]

These attacks, called BGP hijackings or session hacking, intercept data headed to a target IP address and trick the system into redirecting it to another network, such as an eavesdropper's network. Anyone with a BGP router can intercept data headed to a target IP address, although the attack is limited to traffic headed *to* (not *from*) them, and it cannot interfere with traffic within an autonomous system. This type of attack occurs in the following way:[19]

---

[16] Stephen T. Kent, "Securing the Border Gateway Protocol," *The Internet Protocol Journal*, 6, no. 3 (2003).

[17] Bradley R. Smith and J. J. Garcia-Luna-Aceves, "Securing the Border Gateway Routing Protocol," in *Global Telecommunications Conference, 1996. GLOBECOM '96. Communications: The Key to Global Prosperity*, ed. Ole J. Jacobsen (London: Institute for Electrical and Electronics Engineers, 1996), 81–85.

[18] Kim Zetter, "Revealed: The Internet's Biggest Security Hole," *Wired*, August 26, 2008.    [19] Ibid.

When a user types a web site name into his browser or clicks "send" to launch an e-mail, a Domain Name System server produces an IP address for the destination. A router belonging to the user's ISP then consults a BGP table for the best route. That table is built from announcements, or "advertisements," issued by ISPs and other networks – also known as Autonomous Systems, or ASes – declaring the range of IP addresses, or IP prefixes, to which they'll deliver traffic.

The routing table searches for the destination IP address among those prefixes. If two ASes deliver to the address, the one with the more specific prefix "wins" the traffic. For example, one AS may advertise that it delivers to a group of 90,000 IP addresses, while another delivers to a subset of 24,000 of those addresses. If the destination IP address falls within both announcements, BGP will send data to the narrower, more specific one.

To intercept data, an eavesdropper would advertise a range of IP addresses he wished to target that was narrower than the chunk advertised by other networks. The advertisement would take just minutes to propagate worldwide, before data headed to those addresses would begin arriving to his network.

The result of BGP hijacking is that customers would not be able to access the information that they were seeking and would instead receive error messages. According to network experts at Rensys, BGP hijacking "is an exceedingly blunt instrument ... about as subtle as a firecracker in a funeral home – the effects are visible for all to see, planetwide."[20] This type of incident has happened many times, sometimes accidentally, and it is usually remedied fairly quickly.

In 2008, a well-publicized incident of BGP hijacking prevented people around the world from accessing YouTube.com for several hours. The event occurred when Pakistan Telecom attempted to block access for anyone within Pakistan to YouTube in order to censor content that the government deemed objectionable. Pakistan Telecom and its upstream partners accidentally advertised to routers around the world (instead of solely within Pakistan), and for 2 hours all YouTube traffic went into a black hole.[21]

Similarly, in April 2010, China Telecom erroneously distributed a message to block more than 50,000 IP addresses. For twenty minutes, all traffic directed at these IP addresses was sucked into China Telecom's network. Network experts at Rensys concluded that this incident was also an accident, like the Pakistan incident.[22]

Another, more stealthy form of this type of attack, called a "man-in-the-middle" attack, made its official debut in 2013. This type of attack had been known within the information technology (IT) community for years, with a presentation at a DefCon hacker conference in 2008 about how it could occur, but it was not until 2013 that an actual attack of this kind was uncovered. A man-in-the-middle attack occurs in much

[20]  Jim Cowie, "China's 18-Minute Mystery" (Dyn Research, 2010).
[21]  Kim Zetter, "Someone's Been Siphoning Data through a Huge Security Hole in the Internet," *Wired*, December 5, 2013.
[22]  Ibid.

the same way as BGP hijacking, but with a twist. Instead of redirecting traffic to another network, which results in error messages to the user, these attacks redirect traffic to a different network and then forward it on to its intended destination after it has had a chance to view, copy, or change the information. The result is that the messages have been intercepted and potentially altered, but there is no error message, so it does not appear to the user that anything out of the ordinary has happened.

In 2013, someone hijacked traffic sent to government agencies, corporate offices, and other places in the United States and elsewhere. The traffic was redirected to Belarus and Iceland before being sent on to its intended destination. This pattern repeated itself thirty-six times over the course of several months until it was noticed by network monitors at Rensys. The grabs lasted from minutes to days and were done in a way that experts determined could not have been an accident. Traffic was intercepted from about 15,000 IP addresses, and it is unknown what was done with it – whether credit card information had been stolen, emails and spreadsheets had been read, or sensitive data had been copied. Although the traffic was routed through Belarus and Iceland, it does not necessarily indicate that whoever was behind it was physically located in either of those countries. Instead, they could be located elsewhere and the systems used as proxies.[23]

There have been other cases of BGP hijacking, such as in Syria and Indonesia, that were deemed accidental but still affected a large amount of traffic. In 2014, there was a sophisticated BGP hijacking involving Bitcoin, which resulted in the theft of 83,000 US dollars' worth of Bitcoins. In this attack, the attackers even tried to hide the origin of the attack using autonomous system spoofing to make it appear that it came from somewhere else.[24]

BGP hijackings and man-in-the-middle attacks can be mitigated through several different steps. According to network expert Jim Cowie, if all of the 49,000-plus autonomous systems adopted the following five steps, then the world would have near-global coverage:[25]

1. Use a route monitoring service of their own choice.
2. Publish routing policies in Internet route registries and keep them updated.
3. Cryptographically sign their originations and establish chain of authority for every change.
4. Authenticating origins of messages is necessary but not sufficient.
5. Broadly deploy routers that validate route updates.

Until these steps or another solution is achieved, global historical routing data can be used to identify anomalies and chase them down using algorithms. Because we

[23] Ibid.
[24] Andree Toonk, "BGP Routing Incidents in 2014, Malicious or Not?" *BGPMON*, February 17, 2015.
[25] Jim Cowie, "Border Gateway Protocol: The Good, the Bad and the Ugly of Internet Routing" (paper presented at the Stanford EE Computer Systems Colloquium February 11, 2015), 69.

know of these attacks, it is no longer acceptable for them to go unnoticed. As emphasized by Cowie, "BGP route hijacking is an attack on the foundations of the Internet, and there are no simple solutions within reach of global deployment." However, "the incidence of malicious route hijacking can be driven to zero, if everyone commits to watching carefully."[26]

## INTERNET SERVICE PROVIDERS

Internet service providers, or ISPs, are organizations that provide services for accessing, using, and participating in the Internet. ISPs leverage a range of technologies to connect users to the Internet, including computer modems, telephone lines, cable television, wireless Ethernet, fiber optics, and satellite Internet access. In many cases, they own the infrastructure of the networks.

There are different levels, or tiers, of ISPs that have different capabilities; some provide more services than others, and some have a greater reach than others. ISPs connect to each other either in a mutually beneficial free exchange (called "peering") or through buying access to a larger network. Tier 1 ISPs are the larger networks that offer global coverage (for the most part), peer with each other, and do not require connections upstream in order to provide complete services. According to one definition, "Tier 1 networks are those networks that don't pay any other network for transit yet still can reach all networks connected to the Internet."[27]

As of 2014, the Tier 1 ISPs (using Internet protocol version 4) were Level 3, NTT, Telia Sonera, GTT, Cogent, Tata, Sprint, Verizon, Tel Italia Sparkle, PCCW, China Telecom, XO, and Hurricane Electric. This list represents organizations from around the world, reflecting the fact that although the Internet began in the United States and the West, there is increasing activity in Asia, South America, and Africa, particularly as new cable systems are built to improve regional connectivity. Customers in these underserved areas will come online looking for services that are reliable and without single points of failure, have low latency, and are as direct as possible.[28]

DDoS attacks are the primary method of attacks against ISPs. Thus, the next section will explain what DDoS attacks are and why they are so important to ISPs, strategic cyber A2/AD operations, and the Internet in general.

## DDOS ATTACKS

Distributed denial of service (DDoS) attacks are one of the most serious threats to the Internet and cyberspace. While relatively unsophisticated and certainly not new (the first one occurred in 1996 against Panix, New York City's oldest and

---

[26]  Ibid., 80.
[27]  Rudolph van der Berg, "How the 'Net Works: An Introduction to Peering and Transit," Ars Technica.
[28]  Earl Zmijewski, "A Baker's Dozen, 2014 Edition" (Dyn Research, 2015).

largest ISP),[29] DDoS attacks are becoming increasingly more powerful and more common. Today, more than 200 DDoS attacks are observed daily, one-third of all Internet downtime incidents are attributed to DDoS attacks, and a mere 150 US dollars can buy a DDoS attack capable of taking a small organization offline for a week.[30]

DDoS attacks are essentially an attempt to exhaust the victim's resources, such as bandwidth, computing power, and services, so that nobody else can use them.[31] Denial-of-service attacks work in the following way: The initiating computer sends a request to a Web site for information but does not complete the packet-switching handshake necessary to transfer the data, so the requested Web site continues to try the initiating computer again and again, as it waits for a response. This intentionally misleading request ties up the Web site's efforts in a futile endeavor and prevents it from responding in a timely way to other requests.

DDoS attacks follow the same pattern but are multiplied by many hundreds of thousands, or even millions, of requests, which originate from networks of computers that are harnessed and exploited for this purpose. This network of computers is commonly called a "botnet," or network of robots, that have been compromised and can be used for such purposes without the knowledge or consent of their owner. These millions of computers – sometimes called "zombie" computers for their unthinking role – take part in DDoS attacks orchestrated by one person or a small group of people. Botnets are created by criminal enterprises that use them for smaller hacks or malware to gain access to computers. Then, when someone seeks to launch a DDoS attack, these botnets can be rented out for a period of time. At the end of the agreed-upon time frame, the botnets cease to request information from the targeted site(s) and the DDoS attack ends.

There are four common types of DDOS attack: TCP connection attacks, volumetric attacks, fragmentation attacks, and application attacks. TCP connection attacks involve attackers attempting to occupy or use up all of the connections to infrastructure devices such as application servers, load balancers, and firewalls. Volumetric attacks focus on causing congestion by attempting to use up all available bandwidth either within the network or between networks or servers and the rest of the Internet. Fragmentation attacks send a flood of incomplete TCP or User Datagram Protocol (UDP) packets (or pieces of packets) to force the target to try to reassemble the streams, thereby severely degrading overall performance as computing power is consumed by this fruitless endeavor. Application attacks target specific aspects of an application or service in order to overwhelm it. Application

---

[29] Charalampos Patrikakis, Michalis Masikos, and Olga Zouraraki, "Distributed Denial of Service Attacks," *The Internet Protocol Journal*, 7, no. 4 (2004), www.cisco.com/c/en/us/about/press/inter net-protocol-journal/back-issues/table-contents-30/dos-attacks.html.

[30] "What Is a DDos Attack?," Digital Attack Map, www.digitalattackmap.com/understanding-ddos/.

[31] Patrikakis et al., "Distributed Denial of Service Attacks."

attacks are possible even with a few machines and relatively low traffic rates because they target specific applications or services.[32]

DDoS attacks have traditionally been augmented, or amplified, in two different ways so that they can send more traffic, thereby making the attack more damaging. The first is a DNS reflection, in which the attacker forges the victim's IP address and then sends small requests to the DNS server, asking for very large responses. This technique can amplify a DDoS attack up to seventy times in size, making it more effective at overwhelming the target. The second way is Chargen reflection, in which the attacker asks the device to respond with a steady stream of random characters (harnessing an outdated testing system called Chargen), thereby consuming its computing power and degrading its overall performance.[33]

Why are DDoS attacks such a pervasive and important threat? There are several reasons for this. First, there are more and more botnets in the world. As more computers and devices are brought online, more are compromised and become part of the botnets. The larger the botnet, the more requests can be sent to the target site, thus making the effects more devastating. Second, the business model of "botnets for hire" means that people or groups without any computer or technical expertise can hire botnets on the black market. Thus, they are readily accessible and relatively cheap, since they don't require a lot of investment in maintenance and upkeep past the initial recruitment. Third, and even more important, open DNS resolvers can amplify the attack dramatically, making the hiring of botnets unnecessary.

Open and misconfigured DNS resolvers (or recursors) are used to amplify DDoS attacks. These are servers that are available to anyone to resolve domain names to IP addresses, and they are increasingly exploited to launch powerful DDoS attacks. They amplify, or increase, the traffic and thus the power of the DDoS attack.[34] According to *PC World*, "An attacker can send rogue DNS requests to a large number of open DNS resolvers and use spoofing to make it appear as if those requests originated from the target's IP address. As a result, the resolvers will send their large response back to the victim's IP address instead of the sender's address."[35] As a result, attackers can generate an attack with a network of their own that can amplify the attack by one hundred times. Open resolvers are more of a threat than botnets because botnets typically only have modest connections to the Internet (e.g., home servers), whereas open resolvers frequently access some of the bigger pipes of the Internet.[36] The good news is that in March 2013, the list of open resolvers (which had been known to network security firms) was made public in the hopes that the 21.7 million open resolvers

[32]  "What Is a DDos Attack?"   [33]  Ibid.
[34]  Matthew Prince, "The DDos That Almost Broke the Internet," *Cloudflare*, March 27, 2013.
[35]  Lucian Constantin, "Report: Open DNS Resolvers Increasingly Abused to Amplify DDos Attacks," *PC World*, October 25, 2012.
[36]  Prince, "The DDos That Almost Broke the Internet."

online would reconfigure themselves or shut down so that they would not continue to contribute to the problem. However, a year later, the number of open resolvers was reported to be 28 million.[37]

Preventing DDoS attacks is difficult and nearly impossible to do with complete effectiveness. Among the measures that can be undertaken to prevent DDoS attacks are good "cyber hygiene" steps, such as insuring the use of up-to-date virus protection and software patches. Good computer safety steps reduce the likelihood not only of being a victim of attack but also of having the computer become a zombie and participate in an attack. At the network level, systems can be monitored for their "health," and if illegitimate traffic is detected going to or from the network, then steps can be taken to remedy the situation.

Early warning systems are essential for reacting to DDoS attacks before they are able to cause significant damage. Detection can come in the search for patterns (signatures) of attack (or as compared to known attackers), or it can come in the form of examining the boundaries of the normal traffic and seeking anomalies or outliers. Regardless of the early warning systems in place, addressing DDoS attacks requires filtering out the malicious traffic, although there may be some filtering of normal traffic as well in the process and perhaps a temporary increase in bandwidth in order to augment the victim's capacity to continue to function and provide services while simultaneously dealing with the attack.

According to leading technical experts, DDoS attacks can break the Internet by overwhelming it with requests. If these attacks target a site, that site will be inaccessible until the attack ceases, unless its owners hire a security firm such as CloudFlare, which specializes in diffusing DDoS attacks using the Anycast system, which disperses the attack by permitting multiple locations of the Web site around the world and then routing the queries to the nearest data center to the request, thereby mitigating the effects of the attack.[38]

However, a DDoS attack could also target an Internet exchange point (IX). The Spamhaus attackers eventually switched from targeting Spamhaus to targeting the core IX infrastructure on the London Internet Exchange (LINX), the Amsterdam Internet Exchange (AMS-IX), the Frankfurt Internet Exchange (DE-CIX), and the Hong Kong Internet Exchange (HKIX). The LINX was most significantly affected because it had some vulnerabilities that the others did not have. The attack peaked at 309 billions of bits per second (Gbps) – the largest that had ever been seen at the time. The largest routers that can be purchased have 100 Gbps, are very expensive, and are thus not the industry standard (note: the industry standard is 10 Gbps or multiples of that, such as 30 or 40 Gbps). The attack was pushed upstream to Tier 1 providers, but it still had an effect on Internet access, particularly in Europe, where access was sluggish.[39]

---

[37] DEFCON video of Matthew Prince, "How to Break the Internet."
[38] Prince, "The DDos That Almost Broke the Internet." [39] Ibid.

In order to protect IXes, some experts recommend that IP addresses of IXes should not be announced as routable across the public Internet. In addition, packets destined for IP addresses should only be permitted from other IX IP addresses, in order to ensure reliability and trustworthiness.[40]


## CONCLUSION

There are many different ways that the logic layer can be manipulated to cause widespread anti-access situation on the Internet. The key nodes described in this chapter (root servers, BGPs, and ISPs) underpin the functional logic of the Internet as well as other technologies connected in cyberspace. This layer is entirely man-made and can therefore be altered, updated, or manipulated in innumerable ways in order to enhance security or conduct attacks for the purposes of financial, political, or personal gain. The structure of the logic layer reflects the creativity of the technical experts who built and now maintain it, as well as the necessary decisions about optimal functionality, trust, security, and openness. In this layer, it is most evident that the origins of the Internet are rooted in an environment of trust and openness; these characteristics have allowed it to flourish into the ubiquitous global network we know today but have also left it vulnerable to malicious attacks.

The most significant, although rather inelegant, type of attack against the logic layer is the DDoS attack. While criticized by many as being a blunt instrument, according to leading technical experts they are the blunt instruments that can destroy the Internet. The size and sophistication of DDoS attacks have been increasing sharply in recent years; therefore, it is necessary to consider their potential impacts not only on Web sites but also on the critical nodes of the logic layer, where the most damage to the system can be rendered.

[40]   Ibid.

# 5

## Implications for Deterrence and Coercion

Cyberspace communications infrastructure and logic rules are essential to the continued functioning of global commerce, diplomacy, and social networks of the twenty-first century. The previous chapters have demonstrated that strategic cyber A2/AD operations are possible and could deny states access to the benefits of cyberspace. Now that we know this, the question must be asked: What do we do with this information? States can try to protect themselves from strategic A2/AD operations in cyberspace, but can they also use it to deter or coerce others?

The ability to hold cyberspace infrastructure and communication nodes at risk is a significant factor in a conflict environment. Governments rely on cyberspace communications for command and control of military forces, economic stability, and societal well-being. Without access to cyberspace, the economy would immediately come to a halt, with millions of dollars lost per day of non-connectivity. Government, law enforcement, and security forces would have a difficult time functioning and protecting the population from domestic or foreign threats. Societal functioning would grind to a halt as people would need to develop alternate methods of conducting daily, routine activities.

Because of the serious impact of a strategic cyber A2/AD operation for society as a whole, it is likely that it would be applied leading up to or during a military conflict as one element of a larger campaign. At any threshold lower than armed conflict, strategic cyber A2/AD operations present the risk of potentially escalating the existing crisis to the level of armed conflict or broadening an existing armed conflict, as states could perceive the strategic cyber A2/AD action as a threat to their defences, economies, and societies.

Some scholars, such as Thomas Rid, discount the threat of cyber war, and others, such as Brandon Valeriano and Ryan C. Maness, assert that large-scale cyber conflicts are statistically unlikely to occur because they have not yet happened.[1] Yet, these dismissals of the dangers of major cyber conflict are unsatisfying for several reasons. First, just because something has not happened yet is no reason to assume

---

[1] Thomas Rid, *Cyber War Will Not Take Place* (New York, NY: Oxford University Press, 2013); Brandon Valeriano and Ryan C. Maness, *Cyber War Versus Cyber Realities: Cyber Conflict in the International System* (Oxford; New York: Oxford University Press, 2015).

that it will not happen in the future. Based on the historical data, nuclear warfare was empirically unlikely until August 1945. Second, to prevent the occurrence of an action, it is best to plan against it, not ignore it or dismiss it as unlikely. Even though nuclear weapons have not been used for more than seventy years, the United States and others still maintain updated deterrence strategies and capabilities. States must plan and prepare for a variety of possible situations and outcomes, the predictable and mundane as well as the black swan events.

Not all conflicts will result in a cyber war or cyber weapons, but cyberspace is an undeniable enabler to modern military actions and cyber weapons are being deployed more frequently than a decade ago. Cyber actions are yet another tool in the panoply of international relations; as weapons, they will be chosen and used in specific contexts and deployed because of their perceived benefits. Just because a weapon is available does not mean it will be used, but just because a weapon has not been used yet does not mean that it never will be used.

Deterrence in cyberspace continues to be debated, particularly because there is a lack of information about capabilities and intentions of actors in cyberspace, which normally form the basis of a deterrence strategy or theory. Additionally, coercion has been largely omitted from discussions of cyber strategy and conflict, but could provide an option to traditional military engagement and therefore warrants examination. Ironically for a network of networks, cooperation in cyberspace has also received relatively little scholarly attention, but it could provide useful insights into peace-building or conflict mitigation strategies. This chapter examines how theories of deterrence, coercion, and cooperation relate to A2/AD strategies and the implications for strategic A2/AD operations in cyberspace.

### LESSONS FROM NUCLEAR DETERRENCE THEORY

In his seminal 1960 book _The Strategy of Conflict_, Thomas C. Schelling provided a "strategy of conflict" that changed the way scholars, policy makers, and war fighters looked at war. Schelling observed that nuclear weapons changed conflict so that it was no longer necessary to defeat an adversary's military; rather, an adversary could be coerced by holding its citizens at risk.[2] His argument, which threatened nuclear attack on vulnerable civilian populations, served as the preferred policy for US decision makers throughout the Cold War.

In his formula for deterrence, there is an assumption of rationality on the part of the United States and the Soviet Union. Both sides understood the risks, intentions, and capabilities of the other, and nuclear war could be avoided if "correct choices" were made. The threats were successful because each side had an accurate expectation of the influence the threats would have on the other's actions.[3]

[2]  Thomas C. Schelling, _The Strategy of Conflict_ (Cambridge, MA: Harvard University Press, 1960).
[3]  Philip Green, _Deadly Logic: The Theory of Nuclear Deterrence_ (Columbus: Ohio State University Press, 1966), 158.

Despite the assumption of rationality on the part of both the United States and the Soviet Union, there was still a great deal of uncertainty within the deterrence equation. Uncertainty presented "an inherent sense of risk," which could spiral out of control if a crisis escalated to war.[4] As Schelling noted:

> Not all the frontiers and thresholds are precisely defined, fully reliable, and known to be so beyond the least temptation to test them out, to explore for loopholes, or to take a chance that they may be disconnected this time. Violence, especially war, is a confused and uncertain activity, highly unpredictable, depending on decisions made by fallible human beings organized into imperfect governments, depending on fallible communications and warning systems and on the untested performance of people and equipment. It is furthermore a hotheaded activity, in which commitments and reputations can develop a momentum of their own.[5]

Schelling argued that it was the "threat of pain" and not the threat of military defeat that helped to prevent escalation into general war. Notions of military-on-military use of force had been replaced by the idea that civilians would bear the cost of war and the pain associated with it. This threat of pain to be felt by the civilian population was a useful fulcrum in nuclear deterrence that helped prevent the escalation of conflict into general war.[6] Civilian population centers thus became the centers of gravity in a threatened nuclear conflict; the threat of imposing extreme damage on civilian populations was a more potent deterrent than the threat of military-on-military applications of force. The uncertainty associated with decision-making in the fog of war and the potential risk to civilians combined bolstered the deterrence concept of mutually assured destruction.[7]

However, a good offensive strategy was not the only element of deterrence. Contemporaries of Schelling, such as Herman Kahn and Glynn Snyder, argued for deterrence through robust defense.[8] Snyder differentiated between the concepts of deterrence, defense, and denial. He defined deterrence as a process of convincing the adversary to eschew an action by creating a situation in which the costs of the action outweigh the benefits. He defined defense as reducing the adversary's ability to cause damage, if deterrence fails. Denial capabilities affect the adversary's "probability of gaining his objective." He further argues that deterrence is inherently a peacetime activity, whereas defense is a wartime activity that is linked to denial (the ability to achieve objectives).[9]

---

[4]  Lawrence Freedman, *The Evolution of Nuclear Strategy*, vol. 3 (New York: Palgrave Macmillan, 2003), 207.

[5]  Thomas C. Schelling, *Arms and Influence* (New Haven, CT: Yale University Press, 1966), 93.

[6]  Ibid., 1–34; Christopher Wrenn, "Strategic Cyber Deterrence" (Tufts University, 2012), 73.

[7]  Schelling, *The Strategy of Conflict*, 233.

[8]  Herman Kahn, *On Thermonuclear War* (Princeton, NJ: Princeton University Press, 1960); Glynn Herald Snyder, *Deterrence and Defense* (Princeton, NJ: Princeton University Press, 1961).

[9]  Wrenn, "Strategic Cyber Deterrence," 74–75.

Many scholars from the "third wave" of deterrence theory in the 1970s, such as Alexander George and Richard Smoke, argued that the military aspect of deterrence was exaggerated and there was a much greater, unexploited opportunity for classic diplomacy to influence adversaries.[10] This approach was codified in the May 1972 Basic Principles Agreement (BPA) between the United States and the Soviet Union, which established the rules for détente. The BPA provided rules for the conduct of nuclear warfare, but even where it merely reflected a statement of intent, that was significant because it marked a shift in the atmosphere from confrontation to cooperation.[11]

The post–Cold War environment, or the "second nuclear age," presented new challenges to the deterrence theory. Leaving behind the stability of the bipolar system during the Cold War, the current era has nine nuclear-armed countries, some of which are rising powers and others that face grave threats to their stability and security.[12] Moreover, the increase in the number of potential state and non-state adversaries and limited confidence in attribution creates a vastly different – and more complex – environment than the Cold War balance-of-pain construct. Instead of the question of "how much force is enough" for deterrence, the question became, "how much do you know" about an actor.[13]

To that end, deterrence theory evolved even further with the 2006 US Department of Defense Quadrennial Defense Review (QDR), which introduced the concept of tailored deterrence. Tailored deterrence theory focuses on developing tailorable capabilities to deter a wider range of actors, from advanced military powers, to regional military powers, to non-state armed groups or terrorist networks. The logic behind tailored deterrence is that a one-size-fits-all approach to deterrence does not work against the multitude of diverse actors today. At its essence, deterrence is about altering the decision-making calculus of an adversary in order to convince it not to take action. When the only nuclear-armed adversary was the Soviet Union, there was only one decision-making loop to be influenced and thus no need to have multiple strategies. Today, there are many nuclear-armed powers, each with their own decision-making processes that reflect their national goals and political structures. In this more diverse environment, one size certainly does not fit all, as deterrence is ultimately a subjective and psychological endeavor. In order to influence adversaries' decision-making processes and perceptions, the state seeking to

[10]   Ibid., 81; Alexander L. George and Richard Smoke, *Deterrence in American Foreign Policy: Theory and Practice* (New York: Columbia University Press, 1974), 591.

[11]   Wrenn, "Strategic Cyber Deterrence," 83; Roger E. Kanet and Edward A. Kolodziej, *The Cold War as Cooperation* (Baltimore, MD: Johns Hopkins University Press, 1991), 43–45.

[12]   The United States, Russia, the United Kingdom, China, France, India, Pakistan, and North Korea have declared nuclear weapons capability. Israel is widely believed to have had nuclear capability since 1967, but has not confirmed it.

[13]   Wrenn, "Strategic Cyber Deterrence," 89; Keith B. Payne, *The Great American Gamble: Deterrence Theory and Practice from the Cold War to the Twenty-First Century* (Fairfax, VA: National Institute Press, 2008), 305.

deter must have a nuanced understanding of each one's capabilities, values, intentions, and processes.[14]

In the 2006 QDR, a "new deterrence triad" emerged as well.[15] The new triad centered on conventional and nuclear strike capabilities, active and passive defense capabilities, and responsive industrial infrastructure that could produce more nuclear weapons.[16] The responsive industrial infrastructure is necessary in order to secure the long-term viability of the first two legs of the triad – the continued investment, research, and development of weapons technology ensures the future offensive strike capability and missile defense systems.[17]

## EVOLVING DETERRENCE STRATEGY FOR CYBERSPACE

Nuclear deterrence theory helps lay the foundation for understanding cyber deterrence, although there are very important differences between nuclear and cyber deterrence. There are five main characteristics that distinguish cyber capabilities from nuclear capabilities:

1. The nature of the weapons and their effects are vastly different.
2. There are differences in the spatial scale in which actors employ these capabilities.
3. Temporal differences exist in the duration of the attacks and lingering effects.
4. Exhibitions of heroism and bravery are unlikely to be a factor in the cyber domain.
5. Diffusion of decision-making is prevalent in the cyber domain.[18]

These differences notwithstanding, the theoretical underpinning of both nuclear and cyber deterrence rests upon the capability to deter by punishment and denial, and enhance international cooperation.

Cyber deterrence theory has emerged in two waves, the first starting in the mid-1990s.[19] In the first wave, scholars and practitioners such as Richard Hayes, Rear Admiral Gary Wheatley, Timothy Thomas, Roger Barnett, Howard Lipson, and Geoffrey French evaluated the applicability of nuclear deterrence theory to cyberspace, debated the importance of punishment versus denial for cyber deterrence, and examined the utility of cooperation in the new domain. Some scholars, such as Martin Libicki, concluded that given the unique challenges of the cyber

---

[14] Michael Connell, "Deterring Iran's Use of Offensive Cyber: A Case Study" (CNA, 2014).

[15] The older nuclear triad concept was entirely different and focused on the delivery of a nuclear arsenal by bomber aircraft, land-based missiles, and ballistic missile submarines, thereby ensuring a second-strike capability for the United States.

[16] "Quadrennial Defense Review Report" (U.S. Department of Defense, 2006).

[17] David S. McDonough, "Tailored Deterrence: The 'New Triad' and the Tailoring of Nuclear Superiority" (Canadian International Council, 2009).

[18] Wrenn, "Strategic Cyber Deterrence," 100–101.

[19] For a complete analysis of the cyber deterrence literature, see ibid., 99–175.

domain, deterrence was, at the very least, problematic. Libicki outlined five elements necessary for deterrence that illustrated how problematic deterrence is in cyberspace:

1. The incident must be well defined.
2. The identity of the perpetrator must be clear.
3. The will and ability to carry out punishment must be believed.
4. The perpetrator must have something of value at stake.
5. The punishment must be controllable.[20]

Similarly, Richard Harknett concluded that earlier models of deterrence were irrelevant because due to the emphasis on societal connectivity, an attack that destroyed information was not susceptible to retaliation in kind.[21] Scholars such as Stephen Blank concurred with Libicki and Harknett, saying that neither conventional nor nuclear deterrence strategies were sufficient for deterring attacks in cyberspace.[22] These scholars articulated the challenges of attempting cyber deterrence – and thus laid out the path ahead to developing better cyber deterrence.

The second wave of cyber deterrence theory emerged after the cyber attacks in Estonia in 2007 and Georgia in 2008. These efforts focused on real national security challenges, as opposed to theoretical concerns about what could happen. Cyber wars and destructive cyber weapons were a reality that demanded immediate answers, so a second look was given to prior deterrence strategies. This second wave resulted in recognition that some aspects of nuclear deterrence theory were useful, but that ultimately there needed to be new ideas to form the framework of cyber deterrence in a way that meaningfully addressed the unique challenges of the domain.[23]

Scholars such as Joseph Nye, Charles Glaser, Will Goodman, Dmitri Alperovitch, and others acknowledged the problems associated with attribution, particularly the challenges of definitive and timely attribution in cyberspace, but argued that it was not an insurmountable barrier to deterrence. They argued for improvements in cyber policy, stronger national critical infrastructure, active defenses, and other steps that would lead to stronger deterrence by denial.[24]

---

[20] Martin C. Libicki, *Defending Cyberspace, and Other Metaphors*, ed. National Defense University. Center for Advanced Concepts and Technology (Washington, DC: National Defense University, 1997), 44.

[21] Richard J. Harknett, "Information Warfare and Deterrence," *Parameters*, (Autumn 1996), 101–102.

[22] Stephen Blank, "Can Information Warfare Be Deterred?," *Defense Analysis*, 17, no. 2 (August 2001), 134; Wrenn, "Strategic Cyber Deterrence," 118–119.

[23] Wrenn, "Strategic Cyber Deterrence," 130.

[24] Joseph S. Nye, "Cyber Power" (Belfer Center for Science and International Affairs, Harvard University, May 2010); Charles L. Glaser, "Deterrence of Cyber Attacks and U.S. National Security" (Cyber Security Policy and Research Institute: The George Washington University, 2011); Will Goodman, "Cyber Deterrence: Tougher in Theory Than in Practice?," *Strategic Studies Quarterly*, Fall (2010), 102–135; Dmitri Alperovitch, "Towards Establishment of Cyberspace Deterrence Strategy," in 2011 3rd *International Conference on Cyber Conflict*, ed. E. Tyugu C. Czosseck and T. Wingfield (Tallinn, Estonia: CCD COE Publication, 2011).

In the second wave of cyber deterrence strategy, interdependence began to feature more prominently. Nye emphasized the benefits of entanglement and interdependence, whereby an attack on an adversary would also harm the attacker.[25] Richard Kugler advanced an argument for tailored cyber deterrence based on denying benefits of an attack, imposing costs on the attacker, and offering incentives to garner adversary restraint. He identified three options for US cyber deterrence strategy: one based on defensive capabilities alone; one based on offensive and defensive capabilities; and one that combined offensive and defensive capabilities with collaborative planning with allies.[26] Christopher Haley posited a cyber deterrence theory based on the principles of defense, attribution, and retaliation.[27] Jeffrey Cooper introduced a new approach characterized by its emphasis on relationships between actors, similar to those that occur in the financial services industry. Cooper argued that attackers could be influenced and deterred through their networks of relationships, so the United States must create circumstances by which states appreciate the benefits of reciprocity, even if the states are not allies or even friendly with each other.[28] Martha Finnemore, Patrick Morgan, Murat Dogrul, Adil Aslan, Eyyup Celik, Scott Biedleman, Brian Mazanac, and others continued with this line of thinking by drawing parallels between cooperation in cyberspace and arms control efforts during the Cold War. They advocated the creation of recognized norms and an international legal framework to address aggression and the use of emergent technology in cyberspace.[29]

In the time since the second wave of cyber deterrence began, there have been policy developments that have led to stronger US national policy on cyberspace and more cooperative international agreements to govern activities in cyberspace. Despite these improvements, there still does not yet exist a widely accepted cyber deterrence theory, and the United States does not have a credible comprehensive

---

[25]   Wrenn, "Strategic Cyber Deterrence," 130–136; Nye, "Cyber Power."

[26]   Richard L. Kugler, "Deterrence of Cyber Attacks," in *Cyberpower and National Security*, ed. Stuart H. Starr, Franklin D. Kramer, and Larry K. Wentz (Washington, DC: National Defense University Press, 2009); Wrenn, "Strategic Cyber Deterrence," 136–137.

[27]   Christopher Haley, "A Theory of Cyber Deterrence," *Georgetown Journal of International Affairs* (2013), http://journal.georgetown.edu/a-theory-of-cyber-deterrence-christopher-haley/.

[28]   Jeffrey R. Cooper, "New Approaches to Cyber-Deterrence: Initial Thoughts on a New Framework" (McLean, VA: SAIC, 2009); Wrenn, "Strategic Cyber Deterrence," 139–141.

[29]   Wrenn, "Strategic Cyber Deterrence," 141–144; Brian M. Mazanec, *The Evolution of Cyber War: International Norms for Emerging-Technology Weapons* (Lincoln: Potomac Books, an imprint of the University of Nebraska Press, 2015); Martha Finnemore, "Cultivating International Cyber Norms," in *America's Cyber Future: Security and Prosperity in the Information Age*, ed. Kristen Lord and Travis Sharp (Center for a New American Security, 2011); Scott W. Beidleman, "Defining and Deterring Cyber War" (US Army War College, 2009); Patrick Morgan, "Applicability of Traditional Deterrence Concepts and Theory to the Cyber Realm," in *Workshop on Deterring Cyber Attack: Informing Strategies and Developing Options for US Policy* (Irving, CA: National Academies Press, 2010); Murat Dogrul, Adil Aslan, and Eyyup Celik, "Developing an International Cooperation on Cyber Defense and Deterrence against Cyber Terrorism," in *2011 3rd International Conference on Cyber Conflict*, ed. E. Tyugu C. Czosseck and T. Wingfield (Tallinn, Estonia: CCD COE Publication, 2011).

cyber deterrence strategy. Moreover, there are still skeptics and critics who believe that deterrence in cyberspace is impossible or irrelevant.

Rounding out the cyber deterrence literature, in one of its most comprehensive analyses, Christopher F. Wrenn argues that a comprehensive cyber deterrence strategy not only does not exist but also has not been truly posited. Wrenn proposes a theory of cyber deterrence that is comprehensive: A robust cyber deterrence strategy must rest on the triadic principles of denial, punishment, and cooperation. Denial and cooperation share the purpose of denying benefits of an attack (particularly useful if attribution is problematic), while the purpose of punishment is to increase the attacker's cost beyond the potential benefit of a successful attack.[30] Specifically, Wrenn posits that denial is a function of active and passive defense, which require "secure cyber lines of communication, a whole-of-society approach to cyber security, security specialists trained and equipped with enhanced detection and monitoring capabilities to confront continuously evolving vulnerabilities, and the wherewithal to find or buy zero-day vulnerabilities using any means necessary."[31] Punishment requires attribution and offensive capabilities or retaliatory means, particularly those that can be tailored to account for escalation between states with peer or near-peer capabilities who are also engaged in cyber conflict. Finally, cooperation requires tactical and strategic cooperative relationships between states that are adversaries as well as non-adversaries. "Tactical cooperation occurs when actors that are non-adversaries establish relationships to mutually satisfy shared interests and objectives ... Strategic cooperation occurs between and among non-adversaries and adversaries, whereby the advantage of mutually beneficial interaction for all actors exists in developing norms as a prerequisite for reaching international agreements governing cyber war."[32]

## PRINCIPLES FOR DETERRENCE FOR STRATEGIC A2/AD OPERATIONS IN CYBERSPACE

Deterrence for strategic cyber A2/AD operations is centered on the three principles established in earlier deterrence theories: punishment, denial, and cooperation. Each one presents unique considerations, challenges, and occasionally advantages for a strategic cyber A2/AD environment.

Deterrence by punishment occurs when the actor signals that the costs inflicted in retaliation for being attacked would outweigh the potential gains derived from launching an attack. Successful deterrence therefore depends on the actor being able to credibly threaten offensive actions in order to ensure the desired response. In cyberspace, attribution poses a significant problem for deterrence by punishment. It is essential that states have the capability to correctly attribute the attack in order to deter potential adversaries. Without the ability to attribute the attack, there would be

---

[30]  Wrenn, "Strategic Cyber Deterrence," 166–168.    [31]  Ibid., 347.    [32]  Ibid., 348.

no way to punish the attackers. Attribution is difficult in cyberspace, but it becomes more achievable in certain contexts and when traditional intelligence methods are also utilized. However, if strategic cyber A2/AD operations take place during a military conflict, then attribution is no longer a problem.

There is a second challenge for deterrence by punishment for strategic cyber A2/AD operations. Punishment itself may be difficult to achieve precisely because cyber technologies underpin the many capabilities that military forces may use to retaliate. A likely reason for a state to attempt strategic cyber A2/AD operations against a country such as the United States would be to degrade its overall military capacity and prevent it from launching effective operations. As a result, military retaliation for a strategic A2/AD attack in cyberspace may not be a viable option, and punishment may have to come from a source that was not cyber dependent, such as political or economic sanctions. If a state does retain the capability to retaliate through kinetic or non-kinetic means, there is the issue of credibility – whether or not that state is willing to follow through and harm the adversary by kinetic or non-kinetic means. In particular, there may be a question of whether a state would follow through with a kinetic attack in response to a non-kinetic cyber attack, and what the ramifications would be on the broader context of the conflict.[33]

Deterrence by denial is achieved through a display of capabilities that suggest the probability of succeeding in the attack is quite low. It can be achieved by reducing the vulnerabilities through hardening, redundancy, training, and continuous vulnerability analysis.[34] Deterrence by denial has some advantages for strategic A2/AD operations in cyberspace. The infrastructure of cyberspace since its earliest days has been designed for resiliency. While much of the physical infrastructure of cyberspace is relatively unprotected, located on beaches, along railways, and in buildings in densely populated areas, very little of that critical infrastructure is critical by itself. The nodes and cables may be relatively exposed and potentially vulnerable; however, none is singularly important to the entire system.

The infrastructure consists of redundant cables and satellites for private sector communications and military operations. The logic programming of the data and telecommunications was designed to adapt to changing circumstance, specifically to automatically route traffic through an alternate route when the first route is unavailable. This "self-healing" property of cyberspace makes it difficult to cause substantial damage without launching a full assault against the infrastructure.

This type of assault on the physical infrastructure of cyberspace would require substantial effort to target satellites and their ground stations, cables, servers, Internet exchange points, and any activities within the electromagnetic spectrum. The difficulty of conducting this type of assault varies depending upon the target country. For a country that connects to cyberspace in relatively few places, such as

[33] Glaser, "Deterrence of Cyber Attacks and U.S. National Security."
[34] Wrenn, "Strategic Cyber Deterrence," 171.

North Korea, this may be achievable. However, for countries with a greater number of connections, such as the United States, United Kingdom, or Russia, it would be much more difficult to target all of their cables and satellites. The downside of deterrence by denial is that it is expensive to harden vulnerabilities and create (and maintain) redundancies. Many states or private industries may be unable, unwilling, or reluctant to invest resources in redundant capabilities instead of other more profitable ventures.

Deterrence by cooperation seeks to prevent an attack through interdependencies, norm creation, international law, and international agreements. Interdependency creates networks that can be leveraged to influence the costs and benefits of a cyber attack. Norms can create a common standard for conduct that can help keep up with the rapid pace of technological development. International laws can deter, while international agreements can help to regulate cyber matters between and among states.[35] The greatest challenge to developing norms, international law, and international agreements is that they involve, for the most part, lengthy diplomatic processes, while technological innovation races ahead. This is not to suggest it is a futile effort; on the contrary, well-grounded and accepted cooperative efforts will eventually cover the scope of cyber activities and innovation, but there is currently a gap time between the innovation and the establishment of rules to govern the use of the innovations.

Successful deterrence for strategic A2/AD operations in cyberspace requires all three elements: punishment, denial, and cooperation. If done successfully, these elements will work together to increase the costs and difficulty of a cyber attack beyond the desired benefit of the attack. Conversely, if there is little to no real cost to the adversary if the attack fails, then it has very little to lose by attempting attacks.[36] Fortunately, states do not need to deter all potential cyber attackers, only those that can cause the most harm. There may not be one formula of deterrence for all actors, but rather deterrence may need to be tailored to the threat or adversary. For some actors, punishment may need to play a more prominent role, whereas denial or cooperation may need to be more prominent to deter other actors.

## CENTER OF GRAVITY AND TAILORED DETERRENCE FOR STRATEGIC A2/AD OPERATIONS IN CYBERSPACE

In addition, there are other important and interesting lessons from the past six decades of deterrence strategy that can be brought to bear on the issue of strategic A2/AD operations in cyberspace. The most important of these is Schelling's concept of the threat of pain against a center of gravity and how it can be translated into the modern age of ubiquitous communications networks. In planning for the future, tailored deterrence and the new triad offer a path ahead.

[35]   Ibid., 172.   [36]   Glaser, "Deterrence of Cyber Attacks and U.S. National Security."

## Cyberspace Is a Center of Gravity

Schelling's argument for the threat of pain rests on the characterization of popula-tion centers as centers of gravity in a nuclear conflict. A center of gravity is defined as "the source of power that provides moral or physical strength, freedom of action, or will to act."[37] The US Department of Defense cross-lists "center of gravity" with the term "decisive point," meaning "a geographic place, a specific key event, critical factor, or function that, when acted upon, allows commanders to gain a marked advantage over an adversary or contribute materially to achieving success."[38]

Centers of gravity can be difficult to determine, and they can shift with changes over time. In physics, a center of gravity is where the weight is concentrated and can be determined either through a plumb line or by finding the balancing point. Metaphorically, the balancing point in modern societies is where the discrete elements or components of life intersect. It is where government, military, economy, and civil society interact. In the modern communications age, these sectors interact and intersect through technology, specifically information technology that is under-pinned by cyberspace. Cyberspace is a center of gravity because it provides a source of power in the modern environment and it enables the interaction and intersection of critical sectors of the state.

If cyberspace itself is a center of gravity, how can it be attacked or leveraged to gain significant advantage? What is the modern equivalent of Schelling's threat of pain in cyberspace? Since it is not in the interest of most of the world to destroy cyberspace for all users, the threat of pain is strategic A2/AD operations in cyberspace; strategic action that would destroy communications, and command and control; and vital information flows for civilians as well as military adversaries, while simultaneously maintaining it for friendly forces.

Nuclear deterrence theory helps us understand how this threat of pain may potentially be rendered as well as dealt with, managed, and mitigated. First, in order to threaten it, states must possess the capacity to conduct strategic A2/AD in cyberspace. Second, states must be able to deny adversaries the ability to conduct strategic A2/AD in cyberspace against them whenever possible. If this is not possible, states must maintain robust defenses to mitigate the effects of an attack and thereby prevent the full accomplishment of the adversary's goals. Third, in order to bolster credibility and functionally support offensive strike and active and passive defense, states must invest in the research and development necessary to improve cyber capabilities and stay ahead of potential adversaries.

There are some caveats and limitations to the feasibility of this deterrence strategy for every state. By virtue of geography and the structure of networks, some states are more or less vulnerable to strategic A2/AD in cyberspace by other actors. For these

---

[37] "Department of Defense Dictionary of Military and Associated Terms" Washington, DC: U.S. Department of Defense (2015). www.dtic.mil/doctrine/dod_dictionary.
[38] Ibid.

states, the steps described earlier may be helpful but not entirely sufficient unless there is a restructuring of physical infrastructure that offsets the geographic vulnerabilities. Some other states may be more attractive targets for adversaries because of either the weaknesses of the systems or, more likely, their dependence on cyber systems and the state's reputation for advanced cyber capabilities – a successful attack that would be more meaningful and prestigious for the attackers. As US Admiral Mike McConnell, former director of National Intelligence, observed, "Because we are the most developed technologically – we have the most bandwidth running through our society and are more dependent on that bandwidth – we are the most vulnerable."[39]

The interconnectedness of the US infrastructure, particularly its ubiquitous dependence on the electrical system, means that the United States is uniquely vulnerable. "The physical and social fabric of the United States is sustained by a system of systems; a complex and dynamic network of interlocking and interdependent infrastructures ('critical national infrastructures') whose harmonious functioning enables the myriad actions, transactions, and information flow that undergird the orderly conduct of civil society in this country."[40] Within this system of systems, there is interlocking infrastructure that, under good circumstances, promotes the harmonious flow of information and function across the networks. However, under other circumstances, failure within one infrastructure system will not stay isolated and may lead to failure within other infrastructure systems. The very dynamic and coordinated interactions between systems that has allowed for technological growth and development is the precise vulnerability of the system of systems, as it can lead to cascading benefits as well as failures.[41]

This massive interconnectedness of the systems of systems and the interlocking infrastructure that enables modern physical and social fabric of societies is the modern equivalent of, to use Schelling's term, the "center of gravity" for states today. Whether it is through a computer logic attack that manipulates SCADA or other critical infrastructure systems, an EMP attack, or another type of physical attack on the connections of cyberspace, the failure of these interconnected systems could have catastrophic effects on the nation, including government, military operations, economic activity, societal organization, and basic necessities. Anything with that broad of an impact can surely be considered a center of gravity. Our complete reliance on the system of systems, whether by accident or by design, has rendered a new and massive vulnerability.

---

[39]   As quoted in Richard A. Clarke and Robert K. Knake, *Cyber War: The Next Threat to National Security and What to Do About It*, 1st edn. (New York: Ecco, 2010), 145.

[40]   Commission to Assess the Threat to the United States from Electromagnetic Pulse (EMP) Attack, *Report of the Commission to Assess the Threat to the United States from Electromagnetic Pulse (EMP) Attack*, 1.

[41]   Ibid.

Within cyberspace, there are also centers of gravity for the system itself, or decisive points that allow commanders to gain significant advantages over an adversary and contribute to their success. These centers of gravity within cyberspace are a bit more obscure than in nuclear conflict. Satellites that provide access to otherwise isolated locations are centers of gravity within cyberspace, particularly in remote locations and especially for military forces operating out of theater. Important hubs for undersea or terrestrial cables, cable landing sites, and large data farms are also centers of gravity within cyberspace for society, economy, government, and military functions.

As a result of the recognition of cyberspace as a modern center of gravity, strategies for deterrence and coercion for strategic A2/AD operations in cyberspace are more important than previously realized and deserving of greater attention. The other concepts that come from nuclear deterrence theory that could be useful are tailored deterrence and the new triad.

## Tailored Deterrence

The need for tailored deterrence is even more pronounced in cyberspace than in nuclear deterrence. There are nine known nuclear-armed states, as well as several other states and many terrorist and criminal networks that would like to have nuclear weapons capabilities. In cyberspace, the number and type of actors is much greater, which makes the challenge of tailored deterrence even more complex. For example, the decision-making calculus of China is vastly different from that of Russia, both differ from Iran, and all three differ from non-state actors and terrorist groups, such as the Islamic State or Hamas. Complicating the picture even more is that some states, such as Iran and Russia, use other groups as cyber proxies. The use of cyber proxies makes attribution murkier and command and control potentially more difficult and could have unintended consequences for escalation, particularly during a crisis situation.[42]

The simple reality is that different actors can dictate different responses, actions, and counteractions, and cyberspace has a plethora of different actors. Terrorist organizations and rogue states must be considered separately because they have different assets that can be held at risk, different desires to provoke a response, and different motivations for their behaviors. As a result, terrorist groups may be harder to deter in cyberspace.[43] This, however, raises a complex and thorny challenge for a variety of highly nuanced deterrence strategies that evolve in real time.[44]

---

[42] Connell, "Deterring Iran's Use of Offensive Cyber," 9–13.

[43] Lynn, "Deputy Secretary of Defense Speech."

[44] For an example of a nuanced cyber deterrence strategy against Iran, see Connell, "Deterring Iran's Use of Offensive Cyber."

## New Triad

The new triad for nuclear deterrence, and its components of offensive capabilities, active and passive defense capabilities, and responsive industrial infrastructure, can also be instructive for cyber deterrence, particularly in conjunction with a tailored deterrence strategy. Offensive cyber capabilities are the first step in being able to credibly threaten retaliation for an attack and thus inflict pain on an adversary. Active and passive defenses are essential in cyberspace because targets are constantly being attacked within cyberspace. Passive defense is essential, but it is not entirely successful. According to Peter Singer, "97 percent of Fortune 500 companies have been hacked (and 3 percent likely have been too and just don't know it)."[45] Active defenses are necessary to thwart the myriad of sophisticated cyber attacks and intrusions that occur daily.

In addition, a responsive industrial sector, which would include private–public cooperation and potentially a leading role for the private sector, is necessary to maintain and continue a competitive advantage in cyberspace. Because of the rapid technological innovation that occurs in cyberspace, investment in resiliency and redundancy becomes a new, necessary form of denial and defense. Without continual assessment and new technological development, it will quickly become impossible to maintain effective offensive capabilities or adequately defend existing infrastructure.

### THE OTHER SIDE OF THE COIN: COERCION WITH STRATEGIC A2/AD IN CYBERSPACE

The threat of strategic A2/AD in cyberspace is one that countries like the United States must seek to deter but can also use as a threat against adversaries. If the United States can credibly threaten to conduct strategic A2/AD against an adversary, that could be a valuable threat of pain and effective in deterring an adversary from taking unwanted action. The ability to convince an adversary not to attack in the first place or escalate an attack could prevent wars by convincing or coercing the adversary to accede to one's demands. According to Schelling:

> More often, however, substantial wars are won – or prevented – through coercion for the simple reason that it is usually less expensive to convince someone to surrender, or not to attack in the first place, than it is to make aggression or resistance physically impossible. Therefore, in most conflicts against capable adversaries, the primary strategic objective is to make the enemy accede to one's coercive demands, even if this is a demand for unconditional surrender.[46]

---

[45] P. W. Singer, _Cybersecurity and Cyberwar: What Everyone Needs to Know_ (Oxford; New York: Oxford University Press, 2014), 2.

[46] David E. Johnson, Karl P. Mueller, William H. Taft, _Conventional Coercion across the Spectrum of Operations: The Utility of US Military Forces in the Emerging Security Environment_ (Santa Monica, CA: RAND Corporation, 2003), 9–10.

Threatening strategic A2/AD in cyberspace as a form of coercion requires technical capabilities that vary depending upon the adversary. Unlike with nuclear weapons where simply possessing a nuclear weapon and delivery system may be sufficient to deter a variety of actors regardless of their locations or infrastructure, strategic A2/AD operations in cyberspace require sophisticated knowledge of the cyber infrastructure, networks, and chokepoints, plus the technical capability to render key components useless.

Using China as an example, it would be difficult to conduct strategic cyber A2/AD against China because of its vast network of cables that connect it to the rest of cyberspace. The China-US Cable Network, or CUCN, is a submarine cable that links several countries in East Asia to each other and to the United States. With about a dozen major submarine cables in different locations, it would be difficult but not impossible to cut off China's access to these cables.[47] China also has a sophisticated satellite program, which further improves its connectivity to cyberspace. Antisatellite missiles can be used to shoot down orbiting satellites, but there are serious limitations on the effectiveness of this approach for military operational purposes unless a comprehensive, wide-ranging approach were used. It is difficult to hit a moving target in low orbit, and more so to hit a moving target in high orbit. Even if satellites in both orbits were to be successfully destroyed, intelligence, surveillance, and reconnaissance (ISR) aircraft could temporarily substitute some capabilities for a period of time. Attacks at the logic layer targeting route servers, border gateway protocols, or Internet service providers could also be used to deny access in China, although this would likely have a negative impact on other regional players who may rely on the same foundations at the logic layer.

The other way of conducting strategic A2/AD in cyberspace is through a high-altitude nuclear explosion. Nuclear explosions 30 km or more above the Earth can produce EMPs that are damaging to electronic systems on Earth and satellites in orbit. Only the United States and Russia have detonated nuclear weapons in outer space, all events occurring between 1958 and 1962. As such, the United States could credibly threaten China or another adversary with an EMP in order to influence the adversary's actions. However, the drawbacks include the indiscriminate effects of the EMP, which may include destruction of friendly satellites or electronic systems in the general area and violation of decades-old international agreements. In addition, other states may be able to conduct the same type of attack on the United States and thus threaten a preemptive strike in order to destroy the US capability before it can be used.

Diplomatically, the Partial Test Ban Treaty of 1963 prohibits the testing and denotation of all nuclear weapons, except underground. Denotation of nuclear weapons in the atmosphere, in outer space, or underwater are explicitly prohibited, a prohibition intended as a means to both slow the arms race of the Cold War and

---

[47] "Submarine Cable Map." TeleGeography. www.submarinecablemap.com/ Accessed January 6, 2016.

limit the nuclear radiation fallout in the Earth's atmosphere, particularly beyond the borders of the state conducting the test. Originally negotiated by the United States, United Kingdom, and Soviet Union, the Partial Test Ban Treaty has expanded significantly its number of signatories since 1963. Of the 108 countries that have signed, acceded, or ratified the treaty, China is notable for not doing any of these.[48]

In contrast, Iran has fewer submarine cable connections (roughly half as many as China), and all must pass through the chokepoint of the Strait of Hormuz. Iran has not tested antisatellite missiles, but it launched four satellites into orbit between 2009 and 2015, thus joining the club of only ten countries to successfully fly space launchers.[49] The latest experimental satellite Fajr is more technologically advanced than earlier satellites, and its purpose has not been disclosed publicly, but it has imaging and GPS capabilities and was launched from a military base in Semnan province in northern Iran.[50] In addition, there are several other satellites in development in Iran, including Tolou, a reconnaissance satellite designed to spy on Iran's adversaries; Zafar, an imagining satellite; and AUT-SAT, a microsatellite, which are all scheduled to be launched in 2016.[51] Iran is also a founding member of the United Nations Committee on the Peaceful Uses of Outer Space and ratified the Partial Test Ban Treaty in 1964.[52] All of this suggests that Iran has fewer and more accessible connections to cyberspace, thus making it easier to disrupt or deny access.

In North Korea, there is virtually no connection to the global Internet; a select few members of the government and other elites have access to it, but no other North Koreans do. The country has a closed national network, called Kwangmyong, that provides state-approved information, but even this is not accessible to all citizens. There are benefits as well as risks to this configuration for cyber security.[53]

The physical infrastructure for North Korea's global Internet connection is relatively limited (physical infrastructure runs through China, and traffic is routed through China Unicom) and thus potentially more easily disrupted. For example, in December 2014, a cyber attack on North Korea took the country offline for nine-and-a-half hours.[54] However, because there is so little access to the global Internet, it

---

[48] "Treaty Banning Nuclear Weapon Tests in the Atmosphere, in Outer Space and Under Water," U.S. Department of State, www.state.gov/t/isn/4797.htm. Accessed January 6, 2016.

[49] The other nine countries are the United States, Russia, France, Japan, China, the United Kingdom, India, Israel, and North Korea.

[50] Stephen Clark, "Iranian Satellite Successfully Placed in Orbit," *Spaceflight Now*, February 2, 2015.

[51] "Iran Sends New Home-Made Satellite into Orbit," *Fars New Agency*, February 2, 2015.

[52] "Committee on the Peaceful Uses of Outer Space: Membership Evolution," United Nations Office for Outer Space Affairs, www.unoosa.org/oosa/en/ourwork/copuos/members/evolution.html. Accessed January 6, 2016; "Treaty Banning Nuclear Weapon Tests in the Atmosphere, in Outer Space and Under Water."

[53] Andrea Peterson, "How a US Cyber Attack on North Korea Failed – Because Country Has Practically No Internet," *The Independent*, June 2, 2015.

[54] According to Dyn Research experts, the Internet traffic outage in North Korea was consistent with a fragile network coming under external attack; however, it is also in keeping with more common causes, such as power problems. Albanesius, "Internet in North Korea Offline after Apparent Attack."

actually had very little effect. Most government, military, social, and financial networks are not connected to the Internet, so they were not affected by the outage. According to an HP Security report in 2013, "Today North Korea's air-gapped networks and prioritization of resources for military use provide both a secure and structured base of operations for cyber operations and a secure means of communications."[55] Ironically, the country's extreme isolation provides a solid defensive buffer for potential cyber attacks.

Despite its limited connection to cyberspace, North Korea is investing in offensive capabilities and developing its own cyber force. According to a North Korean defector, there is an elite cell within the cyber force, known as Bureau 121, which is comprised of 1,800 hackers who are handpicked from the country's top universities. This group is allegedly responsible for the hack of Sony Pictures in 2014 as well as cyber attacks targeting many South Korean financial institutions.[56] The convenient advantage of the North Korean arrangement is that offensive capabilities are less expensive to maintain in cyberspace than in other domains (building and maintaining aircraft carriers, for example) and provide some plausible deniability; however, because of the country's isolation and limited access to the global Internet, North Korea does not have to invest much money in cyber defenses.[57] As a result, it is more difficult to see how a strategy of coercion that threatens strategic A2/AD operations in cyberspace would have a dramatic impact on North Korea.

Thus, coercion is inherently useful in a dispute, as it can use the threat of pain to preempt the outbreak of violence and convince one side to accede to the other's demands. Threatening strategic A2/AD operations in cyberspace may likely have the desired effect of coercing an adversary to adopt a certain behavior, but much depends on the adversary, their vulnerabilities to A2/AD in cyberspace, and the potential pain or losses that could result from such an action. Some states, such as North Korea, may be vulnerable but the effects of such an attack would not be as devastating as they would be in China, which is less vulnerable, but has more to lose in a strategic cyber A2/AD operation.

The specific advantages and disadvantages of strategic A2/AD operations in cyberspace largely depend upon the context in which they are used, but there are some general observations that can be made. The clearest advantage of a coercive strategy of strategic A2/AD operations in cyberspace is that it may potentially be effective, thereby preventing war. Any action that can prevent war, especially if it does not result in direct casualties, should be considered seriously.

The disadvantages include that it may violate international norms or laws (as well as domestic principles); the ramifications of strategic A2/AD operations in cyberspace will likely be broad, unpredictable, and difficult to control; it will not be equally effective against all adversaries; and the precedent of coercing an adversary with this may open the doorway to potential use against the United States or an ally.

---

[55] As quoted in Peterson, "How a US Cyber Attack on North Korea Failed."    [56] Ibid.    [57] Ibid.

Strategic A2/AD operations in cyberspace would likely violate international norms that are being developed to promote open access to cyberspace. The principles of unfettered access support the goals of creation of a world order that promotes cooperation and interdependence, from which the United States, as well as many other countries, directly benefit. In addition, global communications and the free flow of information across borders can internally weaken authoritarian governments. In these cases, the regime's ultimate goal is to retain control over society and the population, therefore anything that undermines this, such as unrestricted information and communications technology, could become a serious threat to its legitimacy and control. Evidence for this appears in the Iranian, Egyptian, and Tunisian governments' policies of shutting down all or parts of the Internet during popular uprisings, as well as the Chinese government's constant monitoring and blocking of information traveling to that country through cyberspace. Finally, for the United States, strategic A2/AD operations in cyberspace violate the principles of free speech and freedom of expression that are so essential to the American way of life that it may seem antithetical to deny them to others.

As with many other actions in cyberspace, the unintended consequences are of as much concern as the intended consequences. Because of the interconnected nature of cyberspace and the variability in networks, it is impossible to predict with total accuracy exactly how an event in cyberspace will unfold and the impact it will have beyond the intended target. It may not cause damage beyond the intended target, but once the strategic A2/AD action has been executed, it cannot be undone easily, if at all. Therefore, there is a real risk for potential collateral damage that exceeds predictions.

As mentioned earlier, strategic A2/AD in cyberspace may not be equally effective against all states, and certainly has serious limitations against non-state actors that do not control territory. Nonetheless, it may be effective against some adversaries, given the specific conditions and context of the attempt to coerce. However, if the United States or an ally uses the threat of strategic A2/AD operations in cyberspace to coerce an adversary, and other states develop the same capability, then there is the potential for the roles to be reversed someday and this form of coercion could be used against the United States or its allies. The potential for strategic A2/AD operations in cyberspace to be used against a friendly country exists regardless of who uses it first, but if a country has already threatened to use it, then it loses the moral high ground, and possibly legal precedent, if that strategy is employed against it later.

## POLITICAL AND ECONOMIC COOPERATION

Cooperation theories emphasize that repeated interactions build trust between partners, which can have a positive impact on interactions in other areas. Mutual trust mitigates the risk of cheating, which increases the overall benefits and decreases the risks of cooperation. Cooperation is not foolproof though; there are areas where states have differing interests and priorities that prevent them from forming a cooperative arrangement. Cooperation can take the form of military alliances, such as NATO, but, taking a broader look at A2/AD strategies, there are also several strategic approaches that are not traditional military operations.

The United States constantly engages in diplomatic and economic activities that build and strengthen international partnerships, which form the backbone of broader cooperation. Activities such as building international coalitions and partnerships, providing economic aid, negotiating trade agreements, conducting military exercises to build partner capacity and improve interoperability are routine and have the effect of creating broad and deep patterns of interaction that can lead to spillover in other areas, such as cyberspace. This means that the United States, or other globally engaged partners, can potentially leverage diplomatic and economic measures to deter, counter, or undermine A2/AD strategies that are employed against them.

Cooperation, or entanglement, of cyber powers creates an environment that makes agreements more likely and reduces the risks of cheating. Agreements become more likely because the partners have already established broad and deep patterns of interaction that facilitate cooperation in a new area. These existing interactions reduce the likelihood of cheating in two ways: They establish mutual benefits of cooperation, so that cheating will likely hurt the cheater in some way, as well as the other partners; and they provide avenues for punishment in retaliation for cheating or other "bad" behavior.

In cyberspace, existing frameworks for international agreements and norms can be used to foster discussion and generate consensus around emerging issues in cyberspace. For example, the Budapest Convention on Cyber Crime is the most widely accepted and ratified international agreement dealing with cyberspace; this perhaps should not be a surprise, given, first, the long-established broad and deep patterns of interactions among EU members and, second, the fundamental obligation governments have to deter, prevent, and prosecute criminal activities. Another example, *The Tallinn Manual on the International Law Applicable to Cyber Warfare*, is an international effort to develop definitions of and consensus around cyber weapons, tactics, and strategies, by leveraging extant international agreements on armed conflict. Finally, the study of norm theory has also led to ideas of how norms for emerging-technology weapons such as chemical and biological weapons, strategic bombing, and nuclear weapons can shed light onto the process of norm evolution for restraint in cyber warfare.[58]

Economic activities also play an important role in fostering cooperation and undermining potential A2/AD strategies employed against partners. Economic entanglements make it less attractive to states to take adversarial positions against economic partners, since there is a chance that it will result in negative blowback

---

[58] Mazanec, *The Evolution of Cyber War.*

(politically or economically) against the initiating state. Economic integration, high levels of trade, or significant economic entanglements make it more likely that states will eschew confrontation and potential strategic A2/AD operations in cyberspace.

Political and economic cooperation among cyber powers provides many avenues to preemptively mitigate potential strategic A2/AD operations in cyberspace. The establishment of cyber norms, international agreements, and general high levels of political and economic interaction create broad and deep patterns of behavior that can be leveraged to resolve disputes and make conflict less likely. Entanglement and cooperation, however, also make coercion more difficult, as the coercing state potentially stands to lose too. In addition, there is the concern over "lawfare," or the manipulation of international legal agreements for unintended (and antithetical) purposes. Any agreement that may be reached could also be abrogated by nations in the future, if it suits their interest, so there is the classic debate over trust and the risks of cheating. This risk can only be mitigated by threats of punishment for cheating and the continuation of interactions in order to establish greater trust over time.

●

### CONCLUSION

Cyber deterrence theory is still evolving, but nuclear deterrence gives us a rich tradition from which scholars can build. There are elements from the first and second wave of nuclear deterrence theory, as well as the post–Cold War deterrence thinking, that can be useful in shaping a modern deterrence theory that applies to cyberspace.

Cyberspace is a center of gravity in the modern communication age and could be leveraged as such in a large-scale conflict with other advanced countries. Depending upon the level of connectivity within a society, the threat of pain imposed by strategic cyber A2/AD operations could be sufficient for coercion or deterrence. The immediate impacts of a strategic A2/AD attack in cyberspace against an adversary would focus on military, government, financial, and social implications, but given the interconnectivity of networks, it may quickly spiral to have devastating consequences for the entire country and ramifications beyond its borders.

Tailored deterrence strategies are necessary in order to successfully address the decision-making calculation of the myriad actors that could potentially threaten the United States. It bears repeating that not all actors must be deterred, just the ones that pose the most significant threat. Defense, punishment, and cooperation can be used to varying degrees in order to achieve a tailored deterrence strategy for different adversaries. The new triad as it applies to cyberspace is very useful in outlining the steps that any state must take in order to have a robust, redundant, and resilient system that keeps pace with rapid technological innovation.

Cooperation between economic and political partners can also reduce the likelihood of conflict erupting and form the basis for a positive incentive to exercise restraint. The establishment of norms and rules to regulate behavior inside and outside of cyberspace can be beneficial and mitigate the chances of states resorting to strategic A2/AD operations in cyberspace. However, cooperative arrangements and economic entanglements do present challenges with regard to coercion and the threat of strategic A2/AD operations in cyberspace, since it will likely negatively impact both parties.

However, if cyberspace is a center of gravity, then coercion using the threat of strategic A2/AD operations in cyberspace may be successful under certain conditions, although it is not without its limitations and drawbacks. Most importantly, though, it may be successful at preventing the outbreak of war or widespread violence, by forcing a state to accede to the demands of its adversary, thereby winning the war before it is fought. It is for this reason that a declaratory policy that would include as an option of exclusion from cyberspace could be useful and leverage coercion as an option to traditional military engagement.

# 6

# Conclusions and Recommendations

"The most important of strategic lines are those which concern the communications. Communications dominate war," wrote Sir Alfred T. Mahan.[1] Modern
strategic lines of communications are embedded in and dependent upon cyberspace. Protection of these lines and ensured access to them should thus be of
paramount concern for national security. In Mahan's seminal work, he observed
that "war is a business of positions."[2] Just as he advocated over a century ago for
control over the sea lines of communication, today's "business of positions" is
control over the networks of communication. Seaborne trade still matters greatly,
but information and communications passed through global cyber networks is
critical for the modern environment.

## SUMMARY OF THE BOOK

A2/AD operations have a long and rich military history, as the ability to exclude an
enemy from a particular area can be a strategic advantage in a conflict. The principle
behind A2/AD operations is that preventing the enemy from reaching the battlefield
can negatively impact its ability to maximize capabilities and can lead to a defeat,
even if the enemy is the militarily stronger force. US policy has focused on this
concept (under a variety of names) for over a decade, but has not yet linked it to
strategic access to cyberspace, despite consistently acknowledging the importance of
"assured access" to cyberspace as a critical enabler to modern military operations.

Strategic A2/AD operations in cyberspace can be achieved through degradation or
destruction of the physical network and infrastructure that underpins cyberspace.
The physical infrastructure of cyberspace can be degraded and destroyed in a way
that would prevent an adversary from accessing the domain or, if the enemy is
already present, diminish its capacity to fully utilize its capabilities. Satellites and
fiber optic cables are essential to this communications network and can be damaged

---

[1]  Mahan, *The Influence of Sea Power Upon History, 1660–1783*, 144.   [2]  Ibid., 313.

or destroyed by physical assault. EMPs can wreak havoc within the electromagnetic spectrum, thereby interrupting an essential part of the domain. Physical attacks on infrastructure could have short- or long-term effects, depending on the type and location of infrastructure targeted, redundancies within the system, and the type of attack that takes place.

Within the logic layer, strategic A2/AD operations can be created through coordinated attacks on root servers, border gateway protocols, and Internet service providers. These attacks may be highly sophisticated and complex, but they can also be blunt DDoS attacks that are designed to overwhelm the system so that it cannot function. Attacks on the logic layer of cyberspace may tend to have shorter-term effects than physical attacks. This is because the logic layer attacks would need to be sustained over the course of the desired effects, whereas a physical attack could take place quickly and create effects that would last well after the immediate action has ended. Attacks on the logic layer would exploit the very openness and trust that form the basic foundation of the Internet and cyberspace operations.

For those who might want to go further and prevent a country from communicating internally, domestic Internet exchange points and server farms would be the next targets. The decision to stop at isolation or continue to domestic communications depends on the goal of the attack and the broader context. If it is part of a military campaign that is expected to be quick, then isolation would likely be sufficient to degrade military capabilities and diminish command and control. If the goal required a more extensive campaign that would likely meet with significant resistance, then attacking domestic infrastructure would weaken the state by attacking the centers of gravity and accelerate the collapse of the state.

Beyond questions of immediate security, the implications of strategic A2/AD operations in cyberspace are broad and affect many aspects of planning and policy and, in particular, can have significant implications for deterrence and coercion. Because of the dependence of networks on cyberspace, cyberspace has become a center of gravity in the modern era. The ability to inflict pressure or threaten pain through an attack that could lead to a widespread denial of access to cyberspace is significant for modern militaries, governments, economies, and societies. Because the stakes of employing a strategic A2/AD attack could potentially be very high, nuclear deterrence provides some insight into how academics and policy makers could think about leveraging this capability and its potential ramifications. States that wish to deter an adversary from using strategic A2/AD operations in cyberspace must be prepared to credibly threaten punishment for an attempt to do so; they also must have robust defenses in place so as to deny the adversary the opportunity to maximize harm from this type of attack.

Not all cyber attacks can be deterred, and it is simply not worth the investment of time and resources to try to deter all cyber attacks. Instead, threats must be prioritized according to those that can do the most damage. Strategic A2/AD actions in cyberspace would cut off widespread access to cyberspace and disable or degrade the functioning of all systems attached to it; thus, it is a significant type of attack that should be the focus of deterrence. It can also be a useful tool for coercion. The threat of pain caused by strategic A2/AD operations in cyberspace may be sufficient to coerce adversaries into choosing a course of action that they may otherwise not have chosen. The advantage is that this type of coercive tools is non-kinetic, although it would likely have second-order effects that could cost lives, whether through military action or simply through loss of modern technological accommodations. As a coercive tool, it can also be used to influence enemy action, and it can be used to deter, although as with all deterrence methods, it cannot deter everything. Strategic A2/AD operations in cyberspace would need to be tailored as a coercive tool and deterrent for specific threats that are proportional to this type of response.

## ANSWERING THE RESEARCH QUESTIONS

*How vulnerable are states to A2/AD operations in cyberspace, and how can states increase their own security and minimize the vulnerabilities that others may try to exploit?*

States have varying levels of vulnerability to strategic A2/AD actions in cyberspace. For countries that have high levels of interconnectivity throughout their networks, the consequences of a strategic A2/AD attack might be much greater – but they are not necessarily more vulnerable because of their interconnectivity. States that prioritize the development and utilization of technology ideally also have a greater awareness of the risks posed by this technology and their exposure to new and evolving kinds of threats. Therefore, greater interconnectivity does not necessarily lead to greater vulnerability, although a successful attack would potentially be much more damaging. Conversely, poorly connected countries with very little cyberspace infrastructure may be more vulnerable because they may lack the security processes and cyber hygiene measures that can prevent an attack. However, an attack on a country with less connectivity would also render less damage than an attack on a highly connected country.

Through several measures, states can increase their own security and minimize vulnerabilities that others may try to exploit. In order to achieve this, states can increase redundancy within systems, harden infrastructure, create self-healing systems, invest in strong defenses, credibly threaten attribution and punishment, and invest in technological development to stay ahead of threats. They can also engage in cooperative efforts to develop and uphold international norms, establish international laws governing action in cyberspace, and engage in deep and broad patterns of transactions with other nations so as to create diplomatic and economic incentives to eschew strategic A2/AD operations in cyberspace.

*Can denial of access be a form of punitive sanction for rogue regimes that behave outside the boundaries of international norms?*

Yes, denial of access can be a form of punitive sanction for rogue regimes that behave outside of the boundaries of international norms. However, this method poses some challenges. First, a rogue regime such as North Korea may have such little reliance on cyberspace that it may not be a particularly effective form of punitive sanction. Second, it may be difficult to predict or control the effects (particularly second- or third-order effects) that strategic A2/AD in cyberspace may have on a country or society. Given the ubiquitous nature of cyberspace in many countries, the effects may be wider than anticipated and may raise humanitarian concerns. Third, if cyberspace truly is a center of gravity for the regime being threatened, the threat of strategic A2/AD actions in cyberspace risks escalation of the conflict if the regime is unwilling to back down.

Fourth and last, strategic A2/AD operations in cyberspace are difficult to implement and to reverse. It takes time to map the logical layer and create a plan that would affect only the targeted regime, and once logical vulnerabilities are exposed, it may be impossible to use the same ones again. Strategic cyber A2/AD operations would require a host of capabilities and access to physical infrastructure, which may require diplomacy and negotiation with neighboring countries that share the infrastructure and may more acutely feel the effects of a strategic A2/AD operation in cyberspace against their neighbor. Moreover, once the physical infrastructure has been damaged, it can be difficult, expensive, and time consuming to reinstate it and bring the country back online after the confrontation, which may lead to instability that is unhelpful to the goals of the countries or organizations levying the sanctions.

*Can strategic A2/AD operations in cyberspace be a credible form of deterrence? What are its advantages and limitations as a deterrent?*

Assuming that the capability and willingness to follow through on the threat are clear, the threat of denial of access could act as a deterrent in interstate conflict for states that rely on global connectivity, not just for military operations but for economic and social stability. The advantages of threatening denial of access include the fact that it is designed to have a non-kinetic effect that may appear to be more humane or acceptable in terms of human rights and minimizing effects on civilians and avoiding civilian casualties. If it were implemented, denial of access provides a huge technological advantage to the state using it, as it is economically destabilizing, socially disruptive, and potentially debilitating for the adversary's government and military forces.

There is a downside, however, and there are consequences of threatening denial of access to cyberspace. First, the mere threat of it violates the principle of having a free and open Internet or cyberspace, which many countries, including the United States, have proclaimed to support. Second, issuing this threat makes it fair game for other adversaries to do the same in future conflicts. Third, following through on the threat may have far-reaching unintended consequences that could result in blowback or negative effects on friendly countries, since interdependence and trust are at the core of cyberspace.

*What are the appropriate roles of states and private corporations with regard to strategic A2/AD activities in cyberspace?*

As a national security issue, states need to be able to defend their critical infrastructure. In order to do this in a comprehensive way, they must work with private corporations, particularly on threats to the logic layer as well as to ensure sufficient redundancy in the physical network. Private corporations own the vast majority of the infrastructure of cyberspace and many operate the backbone of the logic layer, so their cooperation is essential. In many cases, their technical expertise and access surpasses that of governments, making them invaluable resources for improving security and maintaining reliable access to cyberspace.

The appropriate nature of this cooperation is still being debated and negotiated in most democratic societies, where the issues of freedom, privacy, and security have a multitude of different meanings and vocal supporters. Nevertheless, it seems most likely that the government and private sector need to work collaboratively to determine what needs to be done to protect critical infrastructure (especially from each of their vantage points) and then work together to develop solutions that are satisfying to both communities. Both groups benefit from having ensured access to cyberspace, and there are almost unlimited options for collaboration and permutations of cooperative arrangements to be reached that respect each stakeholder's position and concerns.

*Is cyberspace a new center of gravity?*

The final takeaway is that cyberspace has become a center of gravity in the modern era. US Marine Corps doctrine defines the center of gravity not as a position of strength, but as one of weakness: the enemy's critical weakness. As Clausewitz observed, "A center of gravity is always found where the mass is concentrated most densely. It presents the most effective target for a blow; furthermore, the heaviest blow is that struck by the center of gravity. The same holds true in war."[3]

With the advent of advanced communications technology systems, the center of gravity in modern societies has shifted from population centers to modern networks: the new center of gravity is technology. The ability to hold technology at risk, as well as all the financial, government, and military networks and capabilities connected to it, is as important as holding population centers at risk. Given the

---

[3] Carl von Clausewitz, *On War*, Oxford World's Classics, translated by Michael Howard and Peter Paret, introduction by Beatrice Heuser (New York: Oxford University Press, 2006), 485–487.

extensive reliance of modern states and societies on cyberspace, the ability to deny access to cyberspace would threaten a state's economy, security, and stability. A credible threat against this capability may be sufficient to deter armed conflict or compel a more favorable course of action.

## CONCLUSIONS AND RECOMMENDATIONS

Cyberspace is the new center of gravity, and centers of gravity should be included in all aspects of national security planning. As unpleasant as that may sound to speak of undermining vital communications networks in the twenty-first century, which is seemingly defined by complex networks, global norms, and international efforts to bring peace, it is nonetheless too important to ignore. Underpinning all of the networks, norms, and efforts for peace are communication networks that benefit the users and are susceptible to disruption and destruction. Lines of communication do not just dominate war, but also commerce, diplomacy, societies, and the establishment of the international order.

Strategic cyber A2/AD operations provide strategic leverage over adversaries in war and peace. Given the importance of cyberspace as a center of gravity, deterrence and coercion strategies are appropriate and necessary. Therefore, the first recommendation is to develop a policy that includes deterrence and coercion for strategic A2/AD operations in cyberspace. Nuclear deterrence literature and the nascent cyber deterrence literature have given us precedent that provides a useful starting place: robust defense, credible punishment, and entangling cooperation. The United States is on its way to robust defenses with programs such as National Security Agency's EINSTEIN, but needs to improve upon it and expand defense beyond government systems; credible punishment has emerged in the form of the *International Strategy for Cyberspace* providing a declaratory policy to reserve the right to use "all necessary means" in retaliation for a cyber attack,[4] as well as recent US government actions such as publicly naming and shaming Chinese hackers and retaliation in cyberspace against North Korea for its presumed role in the December 2014 cyber attack on Sony Pictures; efforts to strengthen partnerships, develop cooperative frameworks, and establish bilateral and multilateral agreements are ongoing in order to develop rules and norms for behaviors in cyberspace.

### Toward Developing a Strategy for Coercion

A declaratory policy that includes the possibility of exclusion from cyberspace as an option would be a useful alternative to traditional military engagement. To prepare to use or threaten the use of strategic A2/AD operations in cyberspace, states can

---

[4] The White House, "International Strategy for Cyberspace" Washington, DC (May 2011).

- Invest in requisite physical and technological capabilities and plan to make strategic A2/AD actions a possibility for a credible threat to maximize damage to target state, while minimizing its broader impact.
- Recognize that using strategic cyber A2/AD actions could have humanitarian consequences and consider ways to mitigate the impact of that – or provide immediate relief.
- Consider reversible methods, or attacks that are more controlled, when planning, rather than permanently destructive attacks (such as EMP attacks).
- Consider global posture. For the United States in particular, the new military basing structure in the Middle East and Africa with an emphasis on a "light footprint" might enable the United States to hold more technology at risk because of its greater dispersion. However, as a globally distributed force with cutting-edge capabilities, the US military is also heavily dependent on cyberspace for its ability to sustain operations and power projection capabilities. Thus, it needs to consider its own weaknesses and consider the potential retaliatory efforts or blowback.

### Toward a Strategy for Deterrence

Deterrence against strategic A2/AD operations in cyberspace would require the threat of credible punishment, sufficient denial, and adequate cooperation to be most effective. Each element of the triad has costs and weaknesses associated with it, but collectively they provide for the most robust deterrence. In order to prevent or mitigate the effects of a strategic A2/AD attack in cyberspace, states can

- Deter through policies that threaten punishment, including offensive cyber weapons. States must be able to threaten credible and proportional retaliation for strategic anti-access attacks in cyberspace. The types of retaliation should include the use of offensive cyber weapons, although they may also include diplomatic and economic sanctions, as well as potential kinetic responses that are proportional to the damage created.
- Deny through robust defenses. States must be able to maintain robust defenses that make the effort of a strategic A2/AD attack less beneficial and less likely to succeed.
- Tailor deterrence for specific adversaries, include non-state actors, states of different capabilities and vulnerabilities, and rogue states. Given the sheer number of actors in cyberspace, it is impractical to seek to deter every potential adversary, but tailored deterrence is possible for those actors that pose the greatest threat, as determined by capabilities and intentions.
- Deter through better attribution. Better cyber forensics and non-cyber intelligence can lead to greater success with attribution. Public

attribution and shaming may create a disincentive for actors considering a strategic cyber attack, since attribution makes retaliation significantly easier and these actors may also suffer blowback within the international community.

- Deter through entanglements. States can also deter through economic, military, or diplomatic entanglements that create interdependent interests and outcomes. If a potential action will create harm to, or reduce benefits for, the perpetrator, it is less likely that they will choose that course of action.
- Invest in technology. States that have a technological edge will want to maintain advantage in the cyber arms race until a point at which diplomacy creates a plateau where trust is sufficient that international agreements can be negotiated and upheld.

The second recommendation for policy makers is to invest in resiliency and redundancy to counter a potential A2/AD strategy. This recommendation is particularly important in an era of fiscal constraints and persistent budget cuts within defense departments in many countries. Despite budgetary concerns, investment in redundant and resilient physical infrastructure is a key element to ensuring that all other military capabilities are able to operate as planned. Assured access to cyberspace underpins nearly all activities of advanced militaries. Investment in infrastructure will also have non-military benefits: There is an immediate economic benefit to the private sector companies that make satellites, cables, and server farms, and it can spur innovation and upgrades for government and civilian networks alike.

In order to promote resiliency and redundancy to prevent or mitigate the effects of a strategic A2/AD attack in cyberspace, states can

- Reduce physical vulnerabilities.
  - Increase redundancy in physical infrastructure. This makes it more difficult for a physical attack to be successful and provides more resiliency in the event of an attack. However, it also presents a cost–benefit problem, particularly for the private sector that owns the vast majority of the physical infrastructure of cyberspace but is not charged with protection of the national critical infrastructure.
  - Harden infrastructure. Physical cables and critical electronic platforms and sensitive technology can be better shielded from an EMP attack. Modern societies are more dependent on electronic systems now than ever before; therefore, it makes sense to invest in measures to provide some protection of these.
- Reduce technological vulnerabilities.
  - Continue to create self-healing systems and technologies that can work around problems. These types of systems can prevent an adversary from

achieving the full objective, as well as create resiliency in the aftermath of an attack on cyber systems.

- Protect military and civilian infrastructure, systems, and processes through a variety of measures, including an analog gap in the most sensitive systems.
- Invest (or continue to invest) in stronger active defensive systems. Active defense systems, such as the EINSTEIN program, provide a defensive cyber tool to protect networks from a wide variety of attacks.

The third and final recommendation for scholars and policy makers alike is to define the norms for codes of conduct for states and their citizens to follow. Only through the evolution of norms that are broadly accepted throughout the international community will a stable, self-sustaining arrangement be established; it cannot be permanently maintained through coercion and threats, but rather must come from the values and commitments ascribed to by members of the international community. While states may agree to cooperate with each other at the international level, norms embedded in values and social structures are essential to bring the society in line with the official policies so that states maintain their policies over the long term and effectively deter their own populations from engaging in counter-norm behavior.

To advance international cooperation in cyberspace and form cooperative frameworks, laws, and norms, states can

- Create, abide by, and enforce norms for good cyber practices. Cyber norms may address underlying practices or systems that lead to vulnerabilities that can be exploited for strategic cyber A2/AD actions or norms may include not employing strategic A2/AD actions in cyberspace at all.
- Draw red lines and define what is off-limits for cyber attacks, such as nuclear facilities or water treatment facilities. Given that several states have already issued policies articulating their potential responses to cyber attacks or engaged in actions that make their policies clear, deterrence by punishment is already under way. Further actions by policy makers may include articulating clearly defined red lines, establishing thresholds to issue and carry out threats, and considering retaliation and resistance to attacks.

Norm generation paired with redundancy and resiliency can provide for much great resistance and lessen vulnerability to strategic A2/AD actions in cyberspace. An environment of chronic uncertainty will persist until states agree to appropriate boundaries for cyber weapons and determine what, if anything, should be considered off-limits from attack. International humanitarian law and other international agreements can identify precedents for other types of conflict that may be useful in helping states determine how to regulate and limit this destructiveness of cyber attacks in a cyber-dependent world.

# Bibliography

Aenlle, Conrad de. "U.K. Firm Finds Niche in 'Discount' Satellites." *The New York Times*, June 19, 2001.

Albanesius, Chloe. "Internet in North Korea Offline after Apparent Attack." *PC Magazine*, December 22, 2014.

Alperovitch, Dmitri. "Towards Establishment of Cyberspace Deterrence Strategy." In 2011 *3rd International Conference on Cyber Conflict*, edited by E. Tyugu, C. Czosseck, and T. Wingfield, 87–94. Tallinn, Estonia: CCD COE Publication, 2011.

Armstrong, LCDR Benjamin "BJ." "A2/AD, WWATMD?." *U.S. Naval Institute Blog*, September 2012, no. 24.

Barr, Alistair and Andy Pasztor. "Google Invests in Satellites to Spread Internet Access." *The Wall Street Journal*, June 1, 2014.

Batson, Mickey and Matthew Labert. "Expanding the Non-Kinetic Warfare Arsenal." *U.S. Naval Institute Proceedings* 138, no. 1 (2012).

Beidleman, Scott W. "Defining and Deterring Cyber War." US Army War College, 2009.

Berg, Rudolph van der. "How the 'Net Works: An Introduction to Peering and Transit." *Ars Technica*, http://arstechnica.com/features/2008/09/peering-and-transit/.

Biddle, Sam. "How to Destroy the Internet." Gizmodo.com, http://gizmodo.com/5912383/how-to-destroy-the-internet.

Blank, Stephen. "Can Information Warfare Be Deterred?" *Defense Analysis* 17, no. 2 (August 2001): 121–138.

Blenford, Adam and Christine Jeavans. "After Snowden: How Vulnerable Is the Internet?" *BBC News*, January 27, 2014.

Blum, Andrew. *Tubes : A Journey to the Center of the Internet*. 1st edn. New York: Ecco, 2012.

Carter, L., D. Burnett, S. Drew, G. Marle, L. Hagadorn, D. Bartlett-MacNeil, and N. Irvine. *Submarine Cables and the Oceans – Connecting the World*. In UNEP-WCMC Biodiversity Series ICPC/UNEP/UNEP-WCMC, 2009.

Castells, Manuel. *Communication Power*. New York: Oxford University Press, 2009.

"Chinese Asat Test." Center for Space Standards & Innovation, www.centerforspace.com /asat/.

Choucri, Nazli and David D. Clark. "Integrating Cyberspace and International Relations: The Co-Evolution Dilemma." In *ECIR Workshop on Who Controls Cyberspace?: Explorations in Cyber International Relations*. Harvard University and Massachusetts Institute for Technology, 2012. Workshop paper, http://ecir.mit.edu/images/stories/Clark_WORKSHOP.pdf.

Clark, David. *Control Point Analysis*. Cambridge, MA: Massachusetts Institute of Technology, 2012.

Clark, Stephen. "Iranian Satellite Successfully Placed in Orbit." *Spaceflight Now*, Feburary 2, 2015.

Clarke, Richard A. and Robert K. Knake. *Cyber War: The Next Threat to National Security and What to Do about It*. 1st edn. New York: Ecco, 2010.

Clausewitz, Carl von. *On War*. Oxford World's Classics. Translated by Michael Howard and Peter Paret, Introduction by Beatrice Heuser. New York: Oxford University Press, 2006.

Cole, Harold T. "Warfare in the Electromagnetic Spectrum and Cyberspace: United States Air Force Cyber/Electromagnetic Warfare Command Construct." Air War College, Air University, 2014.

Commission to Assess the Threat to the United States from Electromagnetic Pulse (EMP) Attack. *Report of the Commission to Assess the Threat to the United States from Electromagnetic Pulse (EMP) Attack: Critical National Infrastructures*. Washington, DC: Commission to Assess the Threat to the United States from Electromagnetic Pulse (EMP) Attack: For sale by the Supt. of Docs., U.S. G.P.O., 2008.

"Committee on the Peaceful Uses of Outer Space: Membership Evolution." United Nations Office for Outer Space Affairs, www.unoosa.org/oosa/en/ourwork/copuos/members/evolution.html.

Connell, Michael. "Deterring Iran's Use of Offensive Cyber: A Case Study." CNA, 2014.

Constantin, Lucian. "Report: Open DNS Resolvers Increasingly Abused to Amplify DDoS Attacks." *PC World*, October 25, 2012.

Johnson, David E, Mueller, Karl P, and Taft, William H. *Conventional Coercion across the Spectrum of Operations: The Utility of US Military Forces in the Emerging Security Environment*. Santa Monica, CA: RAND Corporation, 2003. 9–10.

Cooper, Jeffrey R. *New Approaches to Cyber-Deterrence: Initial Thoughts on a New Framework*. McLean, VA: SAIC, 2009.

"The Cost of Building and Launching a Satellite." www.globalcomsatphone.com/hughesnet/satellite/costs.html.

Cowie, Jim. "Border Gateway Protocol: The Good, the Bad and the Ugly of Internet Routing." Paper presented at the Stanford EE Computer Systems Colloquium February 11, 2015.

"China's 18-Minute Mystery." *Dyn Research*, Engineering, Internet, Politics, Security blog, 2010. http://research.dyn.com/2010/11/chinas-18-minute-mystery/.

Crain, John K. "Assessing Resilience in the Global Undersea Cable Infrastructure." Naval Postgraduate School, 2012.

Crowe, Eyre. "Memorandum on the Present State of British Relations with France and Germany." London, 1907.

Dogrul, Murat, Adil Aslan, and Eyyup Celik. "Developing an International Cooperation on Cyber Defense and Deterrence against Cyber Terrorism." In 2011 *3rd International Conference on Cyber Conflict*, edited by E. Tyugu, C. Czosseck, and T. Wingfield. Tallinn, Estonia: CCD COE Publication, 2011. 29–43.

Dombrowski, Peter and Chris C. Demchak. "Cyber War, Cybered Conflict, and the Maritime Domain." *Naval War College Review* 67, no. 2 (Spring 2014): 71–96.

"Ea-6b Prowler." U.S. Naval Air Systems Command, www.navair.navy.mil/index.cfm?fuseaction=home.display&key=C8B54023-C006-4699-BD20-9A45FBA02B9A.

*The Effects of Nuclear Weapons*. 3rd edn. Patuxent River, Maryland: United States Department of Defense and the Energy Research and Development Administration, 1977.

"Egypt Arrests as Undersea Internet Cable Cut Off Alexandria." *BBC News*, March 27, 2013.

"Electromagnetic Spectrum Maneuver Warfare." *Navy Live,* http://navylive.dodlive.mil/2013/
   10/30/electromagnetic-spectrum-maneuver-warfare.
Finnemore, Martha. "Cultivating International Cyber Norms." In *America's Cyber Future:*
   *Security and Prosperity in the Information Age,* edited by Kristen Lord and Travis Sharp.
   Washington, DC: Center for a New American Security, 2011. 89–101.
Fisher Jr., Richard D. "Df-26 Irbm May Have Asm Variant, China Reveals at 3 September
   Parade." *IHS Jane's Defence Weekly,* September 2, 2015.
Flaherty, Mary Pat, Jason Samenow, and Lisa Rein. "Chinese Hack U.S. Weather Systems,
   Satellite Network." *Washington Post,* local section, November 12, 2014. www
   .washingtonpost.com/local/chinese-hack-us-weather-systems-satellite-network/2014/11/12/
   bef1206a-68e9-11e4-b053-65cea7903f2e_story.html.
"Fm 3-38 Cyber Electromagnetic Activities." Washington, DC: Headquarters, Department
   of the Army, February 2014. http://fas.org/irp/doddir/army/fm3-38.pdf.
Forstchen, William R. *One Second After.* 1st edn. New York: Forge, 2009.
Freedman, Lawrence. *The Evolution of Nuclear Strategy.* Vol. 3. New York: Palgrave
   Macmillan, 2003.
Freier, Nathan. "The Emerging Anti-Access/Area-Denial Challenge." *Center for Strategic and*
   *International Studies,* May 17, 2012.
Geere, Duncan. "How the First Cable Was Laid across the Atlantic." *Wired,* January 18,
   2011.
George, Alexander L. and Richard Smoke. *Deterrence in American Foreign Policy: Theory and*
   *Practice.* New York: Columbia University Press, 1974.
Glaser, Charles L. "Deterrence of Cyber Attacks and U.S. National Security." 8. Cyber
   Security Policy and Research Institute: The George Washington University, 2011.
Goodman, Will. "Cyber Deterrence: Tougher in Theory Than in Practice?" *Strategic Studies*
   *Quarterly* Fall (2010): 102–135.
Green, Philip. *Deadly Logic: The Theory of Nuclear Deterrence.* Columbus: Ohio State
   University Press, 1966.
Greenert, Admiral Jonathan. "Projecting Power, Assuring Access." *The Official Blog of Chief*
   *of Naval Operations Admiral Jonathan Greenert* (2012). Published electronically May 10,
   http://cno.navylive.dodlive.mil/2012/05/10/projecting-power-assuring-access/.
Groll, Elias. "White House: The Internet May Be a Strategic Liability to the West." *Foreign*
   *Policy,* February 11, 2016.
"Hacker Vigilante Group Anonymous Ramps up Fight against Isis Online." *CBS News,*
   November 19, 2015.
Haley, Christopher. "A Theory of Cyber Deterrence." *Georgetown Journal of International*
   *Affairs,* February 6, 2013. http://journal.georgetown.edu/a-theory-of-cyber-deterrence-
   christopher-haley/.
Harknett, Richard J. "Information Warfare and Deterrence." *Parameters* (Autumn 1996):
   93–107.
Hyde, Charles Cheney. *International Law, Chiefly as Interpreted and Applied by the United*
   *States.* 2nd rev. edn., 3 vols. Boston, MA: Little, Brown and Company, 1945.
"Icann Factsheet: Root Server Attack on 6 February 2007." 2007. www.icann.org/en/system/
   files/files/factsheet-dns-attack-08mar07-en.pdf.
"International Space Station Again Dodges Debris." *Orbital Debris Quarterly News, National*
   *Aeronautics and Space Administration* 15, no. 3 (July 2011): 1.
"Internet Backbone Withstands Major Attack." *MacWorld.com,* October 23, 2002.
"Iran Sends New Home-Made Satellite into Orbit." *Fars New Agency,* February 2, 2015.
Kahn, Herman. *On Thermonuclear War.* Princeton, NJ: Princeton University Press, 1960.

Kanet, Roger E. and Edward A. Kolodziej. *The Cold War as Cooperation*. Baltimore, MD: Johns Hopkins University Press, 1991.

Kazianis, Harry. "The Real Anti-Access Story: Cyber." *Flashpoints: Diplomacy by Other Means* (2013). Published electronically May 15, http://thediplomat.com/flashpoints-blog/2013/05/15/the-real-anti-access-story-cyber/.

Kent, Stephen T. "Securing the Border Gateway Protocol." *The Internet Protocol Journal* 6, no. 3. 2003.

Krepinevich, Andrew, Barry Watts, and Robert Work. *Meeting the Anti-Access and Area-Denial Challenge*. Washington, DC: Center for Strategic and Budgetary Assessments, 2003.

Kugler, Richard L. "Deterrence of Cyber Attacks." In *Cyberpower and National Security*, edited by Stuart H. Starr, Franklin D. Kramer, and Larry K. Wentz. Washington, DC: National Defense University Press, 2009. 309–342.

Kurose, James F. and Keith W. Ross. *Computer Networking: A Top Down Approach*. 6th edn. Boston: Pearson, 2013.

LaGrone, Sam. "Pentagon Drops Air Sea Battle Name, Concept Lives On." *U.S. Naval Institute News*, January 20, 2015.

Libicki, Martin C. *Defending Cyberspace, and Other Metaphors*. Edited by National Defense University. Center for Advanced Concepts and Technology. Washington, DC: National Defense University, 1997.

Mahan, Alfred Thayer. *The Influence of Sea Power upon History, 1660–1783*. 6th edn. Boston: Little, Brown, and Company, 1894.

Maloof, F. Michael. *A Nation Forsaken: Emp, the Escalating Threat of an American Catastrophe*. 1st edn. Washington DC: New York: WND Books; Midpoint Trade Books (distributor), 2013.

Mazanec, Brian M. *The Evolution of Cyber War: International Norms for Emerging-Technology Weapons*. Lincoln: Potomac Books, an imprint of the University of Nebraska Press, 2015.

McDonough, David S. "Tailored Deterrence: The 'New Triad' and the Tailoring of Nuclear Superiority." Canadian International Council, 2009.

Morgan, Patrick. "Applicability of Traditional Deterrence Concepts and Theory to the Cyber Realm." In *Workshop on Deterring Cyber Attack: Informing Strategies and Developing Options for US Policy*, 55–76. Irving, CA: National Academies Press, 2010.

Mosbergen, Dominique. "Anonymous Declares War on Isis after Paris Attacks." *Huffington Post*, November 17, 2015.

Nair, Brigadier V. K. *War in the Gulf: Lessons for the Third World*. New Delhi, India: Lancer International, 1992.

"Networks and EMS (NES) Roadmap – Navy EW and Cyber Convergence." 2011 *DoD Spectrum Workshop*, December 16, 2011.

Nordrum, Amy. "Hibernia Networks Bets Speed of New Fiber Optic Cable Will Win Customers in Crowded North Atlantic Corridor." *International Business Times*, August 12, 2015.

Northcutt, Stephen. "Are Satellites Vulnerable to Hackers?" www.sans.edu/research/security-laboratory/article/satellite-dos.

Nye, Joseph S. "Cyber Power." Belfer Center for Science and International Affairs, Harvard University, May 2010.

Osinga, Frans P. B. *Science, Strategy and War: The Strategic Theory of John Boyd*. Strategy and History. London; New York: Routledge, 2007.

Patrikakis, Charalampos, Michalis Masikos, and Olga Zouraraki. "Distributed Denial of Service Attacks." *The Internet Protocol Journal* 7, no. 4 (December 2004), www.cisco .com/c/en/us/about/press/internet-protocol-journal/back-issues/table-contents-30/ dos-attacks.html.

Payne, Keith B. *The Great American Gamble: Deterrence Theory and Practice from The Cold War to the Twenty-First Century*. Fairfax, VA: National Institute Press, 2008.

Peterson, Andrea. "How a Us Cyber Attack on North Korea Failed – Because Country Has Practically No Internet." *The Independent*, June 2, 2015.

Prince, Matthew. "The Ddos That Almost Broke the Internet." *Cloudflare*, March 27, 2013.

"Quadrennial Defense Review Report." U.S. Department of Defense, Washignton, DC, 2006.

Rattray, Gregory J. *Strategic Warfare in Cyberspace*. Cambridge, MA: MIT Press, 2001.

Rid, Thomas. *Cyber War Will Not Take Place*. New York: Oxford University Press, 2013.

"Root Servers." Internet Assigned Numbers Authority (IANA), www.iana.org/domains/root/ servers.

"Root Servers Technical Operations Assn." www.root-servers.org/.

Russell, Alison Lawlor. "Cyber and Naval Strategy." In *Routledge Handbook of Naval Strategy and Security*, edited by Joachim Krause and Sebastian Bruns: New York, NY: Routledge, 2015. 189–201.

*Cyber Blockades*. Washington, DC: Georgetown University Press, 2014.

Saffo, Paul. "Disrupting Undersea Cables: Cyberspace's Hidden Vulnerability." International Relations and Security Network (ISN), www.isn.ethz.ch/Digital-Library/Articles/Detail/ ?id=162869.

Schelling, Thomas C. *Arms and Influence*. New Haven, CT: Yale University Press, 1966.

*The Strategy of Conflict*. Cambridge, MA: Harvard University Press, 1960.

Schmitt, Michael, ed. *The Tallinn Manual on the International Law Applicable to Cyber Warfare*. New York, NY: Cambridge University Press, 2013.

Schwartz, Norton A. and Jonathan W. Greenert. "Air-Sea Battle." *The American Interest* February 20, 2012.

Sechrist, Michael. "New Threats, Old Technology: Vulnerabilities in Undersea Communications Cable Network Management Systems." Belfer Discussion Paper, No. 2012-03, Harvard Kennedy School, February 2012.

Secretary, Office of the Press. "Factsheet: Cybersecurity National Action Plan." news release, February 9, 2016, www.whitehouse.gov/the-press-office/2016/02/09/fact-sheet-cybersecurity-national-action-plan.

Singer, P. W. *Cybersecurity and Cyberwar: What Everyone Needs to Know*. Oxford; New York: Oxford University Press, 2014.

Smith, Bradley R. and J. J. Garcia-Luna-Aceves. "Securing the Border Gateway Routing Protocol." In *Global Telecommunications Conference, 1996. GLOBECOM '96. 'Communications: The Key to Global Prosperity*, Edited by Ole J. Jacobsen. 81–85. London: Institute for Electrical and Electronics Engineers, 1996.

Snyder, Glynn Herald. *Deterrence and Defense*. Princeton, NJ: Princeton University Press, 1961.

Sontag, Sherry, Christopher Drew, and Annette Lawrence Drew. *Blind Man's Bluff : The Untold Story of American Submarine Espionage*. New York: Public Affairs, 1998.

"Submarine Cable Map." *TeleGeography*, www.submarinecablemap.com/.

Tangredi, Sam J. *Anti-Access Warfare: Countering A2/AD Strategies*. Annapolis, MD: Naval Institute Press, 2013. www.whitehouse.gov/sites/default/files/rss_viewer/international_ strategy_for_cyberspace.pdf.

Toonk, Andree. "Bgp Routing Incidents in 2014, Malicious or Not?" *BGPMON*, February 17, 2015.

"Treaty Banning Nuclear Weapon Tests in the Atmosphere, in Outer Space and under Water." U.S. Department of State, www.state.gov/t/isn/4797.htm.

U.S. Department of Defense. "Joint Publication 3–13.1 Electronic Warfare." edited by U.S. Department of Defense, January 25, 2007. www.usna.edu/Training/_files/documents/References/2C%20MQS%20References/Joint%20Publication%203-13-1%20Electronic%20Warfare.pdf.

"Department of Defense Dictionary of Military and Associated Terms." Washington, DC: U.S. Department of Defense 2015. www.dtic.mil/doctrine/dod_dictionary/.

"Joint Publication (JP) 3–12, Cyberspace Operations." Washington, DC: U.S. Department of Defense 2013. www.dtic.mil/doctrine/new_pubs/jp3_12R.pdf.

"Sustaining U.S. Global Leadership: Priorities for 21st Century Defense." Washington, DC: U.S. Department of Defense 2012. http://archive.defense.gov/news/Defense_Strategic_Guidance.pdf.

U.S. Department of Defense. "Joint Operational Access Concept." 2012.

U.S. Department of Homeland Security. "Characteristics and Common Vulnerabilities Infrastructure Category: Cable Landing Stations." Draft – Version 1, January 15, 2004.

Valeriano, Brandon and Ryan C. Maness. *Cyber War Versus Cyber Realities: Cyber Conflict in the International System.* Oxford; New York: Oxford University Press, 2015.

Vixie, Paul, Gerry Sneeringer, and Mark Schliefer. "Events of 21-Oct-2002." November 24, 2002.

"What Are Root Name Servers?" Netnod, www.netnod.se/what-are-root-name-servers.

"What Is a Ddos Attack?" Digital Attack Map, www.digitalattackmap.com/understanding-ddos/.

The White House. "International Strategy for Cyberspace." Washington, DC, May 2011. www.whitehouse.gov/sites/default/files/rss_viewer/international_strategy_for_cyberspace.pdf.

William J. Lynn. "Deputy Secretary of Defense Speech: Remarks on the Department of Defense Cyber Strategy." *News Release,* July 14, 2011, http://archive.defense.gov/speeches/speech.aspx?speechid=1593.

Work, Robert O. *The Challenge of Maritime Transformation: Is Bigger Better?* Washington, DC: Center for Strategic and Budgetary Assessments, 2002.

Wrenn, Christopher. "Strategic Cyber Deterrence." Tufts University, 2012.

Zetter, Kim. "Revealed: The Internet's Biggest Security Hole." *Wired,* August 26, 2008.

"Someone's Been Siphoning Data through a Huge Security Hole in the Internet." *Wired,* December 5, 2013.

Zmijewski, Earl. "A Baker's Dozen, 2014 Edition." *Dyn Research,* 2015.

# Index

A2/AD attacks. *See* strategic A2/AD attacks
A2/AD operations
  air use of, 14–15
  definition of, 2
  history of, 11–12
  land use of, 14
  limitations of, 15–16
  maritime use of, 13
  space and cyberspace as increasingly important and contested domains in, 4
A2/AD operations in cyberspace, 21–24
  considerations in US use of, 22
  denying state access to cyberspace as part of, 2
  deterrence theory and, 9
  evolving concept of, 3
  four layers in cyberspace global grid and, 5
  gaps in knowledge about, 8–9
  increasing importance of space and cyberspace in, 4
  Joint Concept for Access and Maneuver in the Global Commons with, 3
  layers and vulnerabilities for, 5–8
  national security and, 4
  overview of, 21–24
  planning and policy implications of, 7
  possible negative effects of, 22
  range of states engaging in, 12
  research questions on, 9, 76
  strategic level in, 4
  tactical level in, 4
  two levels in, 4
A2/AD operations in other domains
  A2/AD strategy incorporating assessment of, 2
  joint operations in, 3, 16, 17
  tactical level of cyber A2/AD attacks on, 4
A2/AD strategy
  advantages of, 69
  anti-access warfare in other domains and, 2

coercion in, 66–70
concept of, 22
contingency planning for and against in, 3
definition of, 4
disadvantages of, 69
historical focus of research on, 3
history of, 11–12
lack of research on, 4
legal considerations on, 23–24
primary missions of US armed forces and, 20
research questions on, 9, 76
tactical cyber A2/AD contrasted with, 4
threat of pain used in, 63
US policy against militarization of cyberspace in, 2
A2/AD, coining of term, 18
access denial. *See* denial of access
aerial blockades, 24
Afghanistan, wars in, 18
Africa
  Internet connectivity in, 48
  military basing structure in, 80
air A2/AD operations, 2, 14–15, *See also* A2/AD operations in other domains
Air Force
  Air Sea Battle (ASB) concept of, 18
  CHAMP ruise missiles of, 36
Air Sea Battle (ASB), 16, 18, 21
Algeria, cable damage from earthquake in, 29
Alperovitch, Dmitri, 58
Amsterdam Internet Exchange (AMS-IX), 51
Anonymous (cyber vigilante group), 22
anti-access
  area denial contrasted with, 3
  definition of, 3
  history of, 11–12
  land A2/AD operations as, 14
  naval blockades as, 3, 13, 23, 24

anti-access (cont.)
  US power project against challenge from, 20
  US strategy focus on, 16
anti-access and area denial operations. *See* A2/AD
  operations
anti-access and area denial strategy. *See* A2/AD
  strategy
anti-access networks, 17
anti-access warfare
  A2/AD strategy and investigation of, 2
  anti-access in, 3
  area denial in, 3
  goal of, 3
  historical focus of research on, 3
  overview of, 2–3
anti-satellite missiles, 32, 67
anti-ship ballistic missiles (ASBMs), 19
Anycast technology, 44, 51
application attacks, in denial of serrvice, 49
area denial
  anti-access contrasted with, 3
  definition of, 3
  land A2/AD operations as, 14
  naval blockades in, 13
  no-fly zone as example of, 3
  US power project against challenge from, 20
  US strategy focus on, 16
Aslan, Adil, 59
assumption of rationality, in nuclear weapons use, 54
attribution problems, in deterrence strategy, 58,
      60, 61
Autonomous Systems (ASes), 46
AUT-SAT (Iranian microsatellite), 68

balancing point, 63
Barnett, Roger, 57
Basic Principles Agreement (BPA), 56
BGP hijackings, 45–48
Biedleman, Scott, 59
biological weapons, 71
Bitcoin, 47
Blank, Stephen, 58
blockades
  aerial, 24
  cyber, 1, 22, 23, 24
  international law on, 23
  naval, 3, 13, 23, 24
border gateway protocols (BGPs), 45–48
  basic components of, 45
  cyber attacks (hijackings) of, 45–48
  definition of, 45
  types of, 45
  vulnerabilities of, 45
border routers, in BGP system, 45, 47

Bosnia, no-fly zones used against, 15
botnets, 43, 44, 49, 50
botnets for hire model, 50
Boydm John, 4
Budapest Convention on Cyber Crime, 71
buffer zones, 12
Bureau 121 (North Korea cyber force), 69

cables, 26–31
  coaxial, 27
  fiber optic. *See* fiber optic cables
  submarine. *See* submarine cables
  terrestrial. *See* terrestrial cables
Celik, Eyyup, 59
Center for Strategic and Budgetary Assessments, 17
center of gravity, cyberspace as, 8, 10, 22, 63–65, 72
centers of gravity
  civilian populations in warfare as, 55
  difficulty of determining, 63
  questions about A2/AD operations in cyberspace
      and, 8
  systems and infrastructure as part of, 65
  tailored deterrence using, 72
  threat of pain against, 62
Challenge of Maritime Transformation
  Is Bigger Better?, The (Work), 17
CHAMP cruise missiles, 36
Chargen reflection, in denial of service, 50
chemical weapons, 71
China
  antisatellite missiles of, 32, 67
  anti-ship ballistic missiles of, 19
  asymmetic means used to counter
      US approaches to, 20
  counter A2/AD strategies needed against, 18
  difficulty of conducting strategic A2/AD against,
      67, 69
  government monitoring of Internet in, 70
  hacking into US weather satellites by, 33
  naming and shaming of hackers in, 79
  North Korean global internet connectivity
      through, 68
  Partial Test Ban Treaty (1963) and, 68
  possibility of using EMP threat against, 67
  submarine cable network of, 67
  tailored deterrence against, 65
  weather sataellites of, 32, 33
China Telecom, 46, 48
China Unicom, 68
China-US Cable Network (CUCN), 67
civilian populations
  as centers of gravity in nuclear conflict, 63
  strategy of conflict and, 54
  threat of pain to, 55

Clausewitz, Carl von, 78
CloudFlare, 51
coaxial cables, 27
coercion
    A2/AD strategy
        coercion as form of, 66–70
    blockades used for, 15
    coercing state as possible loser in, 72
    earlier warfare use of, 66
    importance of strategies against, 65
    need for policy on use of, 79
    norms for codes of conduct needed instead of, 82
    nuclear explosions
        and, 67
    questions about A2/AD operations and use of, 7,
        8, 54, 69, 70, 73
    situations for successful use of, 73
    technical capabilities needed for, 67
    threat of pain used as, 72, 76
    threat of pain used with, 69
Cold War, 16, 27, 36, 54, 56, 59, 67
command of the sea, 13
computer viruses, 30, 51
computer worms, 6, 30, 51
computers
    distributed denial of service (DDoS) attacks
        using, 49
    EMP threats to, 38
    Internet service providers and, 48
    physical layer of cyberspace with, 5, 26
Cooper, Jeffrey, 59
cooperation
    differing interests and priorities of states
        complicating, 70
    in deterrence, 60, 62
    political and economic, 70–72
Cosmos 2251 satellite, 33
counter-A2/AD operations, 12, 20
Cowie, Jim, 47, 48
criminal enterprises, 49, 65, 71
Crowe, Sir Eyre, 12
CUCN (China-US Cable Network), 67
cyber A2/AD. *See* A2/AD operations in cyberspace
cyber attacks
    digital, 7, 8
    electromagnetic, 7
    Estonia, 58
    frequency of, 8
    Georgia, 58
    international relations and use of, 54
    mechanical, 7
    North Korea, 1, 68
    secondary effect of, 23
    Sony Pictures, 1, 69, 79

South Korea, 69
strategic. *See* strategic A2/AD attacks
types of, 7
cyber blockades, 1, 22, 23, 24
cyber proxies, 65
cyber security
    need for US policy to address challenges in, 21
    US 2017 budget on investment in, 21
cyber strategy
    coercion as part of, 54
cyber warfare
    disagreements about threat of, 53
    international law on, 25
    US projection of power to avoid, 20
cyberspace
    anti-access and area denial operations in. *See*
        A2/AD operations
    anti-access and area denial strategy in. *See*
        A2/AD strategy
    definitions of, 1
    denying state access to as part of A2/AD
        operations, 2
    digital attacks on, 7, 8
    electromagnetic attacks on, 7
    four layers of, 5, 7
    global commons approach to, 22
    global grid organization of, 5
    human interactions and vulnerability of, 7
    importance as contested domain in A2/AD, 4
    Information Age and accessibility of, 1
    information layer of, 5, 6
    logical layer of, 5, 6, 7
    mechanical attacks on, 7
    military actions enabled by, 54
    need for greater understanding of, 5
    new center of gravity in, 8, 10, 22, 63–65, 72
    overlapping of layers and types of attacks in, 7
    physical layer of, 5–6, 7
    primary missions of US armed forces in, 20
    protecting layers to maintain full operational
        capacity of, 7
    types of attacks on, 7
    US policy against militarizing, 2
    user layer of, 5, 6
    vulnerabilities to strategic A2/AD attack on, 7
    vulnerability from proliferation of and
        dependence on, 4
Cyberspace National Action Plan, 21
Cyberspace Operations (Department of Defense
    Joint Publication (JP) 3–12), 20

Daniel, Michael, 21
DDoS. *See* distributed denial of service (DDoS)
    attacks

decisive point, 63
DefCon hacker conference (2008), 46
defensive strategy, A2.AD as, 12
denial of access
    current US policy on, 23
    potential enemy uses of, 18
    questions about threat of use of, 8
    reluctance to discuss possibility of, 8
denial of service. *See* distributed denial of service
    (DDoS) attacks
denial, in deterrence, 60, 61, 62
Department of Defense (DoD)
    center of gravity in deterrence and, 63
    cyber defense emphasized by, 2
    cyberspace as operational domain and, 2
    EM spectrum-cyberspace intersection and, 34
    importance of cyberspace in national security
        and, 4, 19
    Joint Operational Access Concept (JOAC)
        from, 19
    Quadrennial Defense Review (QDR) of, 56, 57
détente, 56
deterrence
    continuing debates over use of, 54
    cooperation in, 60, 62
    denial in, 60, 61, 62
    elements necessary for, 58
    problematic aspects of, for cyberspace, 58
    punishment in, 60, 62
    questions about A2/AD operations in cyberspace
        and use of, 8
deterrence strategy
    attribution problems in, 58, 60, 61
    center of gravity in, 62
    differences between cyber and nuclear
        capabilities and, 57
    evolution of, for cyberspace, 57–60
    interdependence and, 59
    lack of information for, 54
    need for comprehensive approach to, 60
    new triad and, 66
    tailored deterrence in, 59
    threat of pain in, 62
    three options for, 59
deterrence theory
    A2/AD operations in cyberspace and, 9
    defense, attribution, and retaliation in, 59
    first wave of, 57
    lessons for nuclear deterrence for, 54–57
    new deterrence triad in, 57
    nuclear weapons and. *See* nuclear deterrence
    post–Cold War environment challenges to, 56
    relationships between actors in, 59
    second wave of, 58

tailored deterrence and, 56
    third wave of, 56
    three principles in, 60
DF-26 anti-ship ballistic missiles (ASBMs), 19
digital cyber attacks, 7, 8
directed energy weapons, 36
distributed denial of service (DDoS) attacks, 48–52
    as pervasive and important threats, 50
    augmented or amplified, 50
    botnets used with, 49, 51
    common types of, 49
    early warning systems for, 51
    how they work, 49
    impact on Internet of, 51
    Internet service providers (ISPs) and, 48
    number of, 48
    open resolvers in, 50
    preventing, 51
DNS. *See* domain name systems
DNS reflection, in denial of service, 50
DoD. *See* Department of Defense
Dogrul, Murat, 59
domain name systems (DNS)
    human interactions and vulnerability of, 7
    logic layer of cyberspace with, 6, 40
    root servers and, 41
    safeguards to protect, 6
    web addresses on, 41
doomsday scenarios, 37

early warning systems, in distributed denial of
        service (DDoS) attacks, 51
earthquakes, 29, 33, 44
East Asia
    counter A2/AD strategies needed against, 18
    submarine cables linking countries in, 67
economic activities, and cooperation, 71
Egypt
    attack on undersea cable off, 27
    government monitoring of Internet in, 70
EINSTEIN program (National Security Agency),
        79, 82
electric power grids, EMP threats to, 37, 38
electromagnetic (EM) spectrum, 33–34
    as constituent part of cyberspace, 26, 33, 34
    continuing evolution of threats to, 35
    control of information in warfare dependent
        on, 36
    cyber dependency on, 34–36
    intersection of cyberspace operations, electronic
        warfare, and management operations
        within, 34
    military use of, 34
    range of frequencies in, 33

electromagnetic cyber attacks, 7, 36
electromagnetic pulse (EMP) attacks, 7, 36–38
  cyberspace connections and, 64
  electronic systems and, 36, 37, 39, 67, 81
  mechanism of, 37
  national security and, 36
  nuclear weapons used in, 38
  popular awareness about, 37
  protecting against, 7
  shielding from, 81
  threat to United States from, 36
electronic systems
  EMP attacks on, 36, 37, 39, 67, 81
  protection for, 38
electronic warfare (EW), 20, 34
EM spectrum. *See* electromagnetic (EM) spectrum
EMP attacks. *See* electromagnetic pulse (EMP)
  attacks
Estonia, cyber attacks (2007) in, 58
Ethernet, 48
Eutelsat, 31
explosives, in EMP attacks, 37
external BGPs (eBGPs), 45

Fajr (Iranian experimental satellite), 68
Federal Bureau of Investigation, 1
Federal Communications Commission (FCC), 31
fiber optic cables
  DNS reliance on, 6
  landing sites as single points of risk for, 5
  operating systems of, 6
  physical layer of cyberspace with, 5, 26
  telecommunications systems using, 26
  vulnerabilities of using, 5
Finnemore, Martha, 59
Forstchen, William R., 37
fragmentation attacks, in denial of service, 49
Frankfurt Internet Exchange (DE-CIX), 51
freedom of communication, 22
freedom of navigation, 12
freedom of speech, 22, 70
French, Geoffrey, 57
frequencies
  EMP attack across broad spectrum of, 38
  jamming of, 7, 24, 25, 34

geographic access denial, 18
geographic features, and A2/AD operations, 12, 13,
  14, 24
George, Alexander, 56
Georgia, cyber attacks (2008) in, 58
Glaser, Charles, 58
global commons, 7, 22

global positioning systems (GPS), 18, 68
Goodman, Will, 58
GPS, 18, 68
Greek city-states, 11, 13, 14
Greenert, Jonathan, 36
ground stations, satellite, 29, 33, 61
guerrilla warfare, 14

hackers and hacking
  BGP system and, 45
  botnets and, 49
  Chinese, 79
  domain name systems (DNS) and, 6
  Internet communications and, 6, 40, 46
  North Korean, 69
  number of companies affected by, 66
  publicly naming and shaming participants
    in, 79
  satellites and, 32, 33
  Sony Pictures attack (2014) and, 69
Haley, Christopher, 59
Hamas, 65
Harknett, Richard, 58
Hayes, Richard, 57
Herodotus, 11
hijackings, in BGP system, 45–48
Hong Kong Internet Exchange (HKIX), 51
Hormuz, Strait of, 13, 68
HP Security report, 69
humanitarian consequences, of strategic cyber
  A2/AD actions, 80
humanitarian disasaters, after cyber warfare, 39, 77
humanitarian relief operations, 15, 23

imaging satellites, 4, 68
Information Age, 1
information layer of cyberspace, 5, 6
information operation attacks, 18
insurgencies, 14
intelligence gathering operations, 3, 22, 23, 61,
  67, 80
intelligence, surveillance, and reconnaissance
  (ISR) aircraft, 67
IntelSat, 31
interdependencies, in deterrence, 62
internal BGPs (iBGPs), 45
International Group of Experts, 24
international law
  A2/AD strategy consistent with, 12, 23, 25, 76
  deterrence by cooperation and, 62
international political events, impact on A2/AD
  strategy of, 16
International Space Station, 33

*International Strategy for Cyberspace* (White House), 79
Internet
 cyberspace much bigger than, 1
 distributed denial of service (DDoS) attacks' impact on, 51
 DNS safeguards and, 6
 government's monitoring of, 70
 popular uprisings using, 70
 strategic A2/AD attacks focused on, 7
 web addresses on, 41
Internet Assigned Numbers Authority (IANA), 41
Internet Corporation for Names and Numbers (ICANN), 41, 43
Internet exchange points, 26, 51, 61, 75
Internet service providers (ISPs), 48
 DDoS attacks on, 48
 function of, 48
 human interactions and vulnerability of, 7
 levels or tiers of, 48
intrusion of systems, 7, 66
Iran
 asymmetric means used to counter US approaches to, 20
 satellites of, 68
 submarine cable connections in, 68
 tailored deterrence against, 65
Iraq
 no-fly zones used against, 15
 skill sets for wars in, 18
Iridium 33 satellite, 33
Islamic State, 22, 65
ISPs. *See* Internet service providers (ISPs)

jamming, 7, 24, 25, 34
Joint Concept for Access and Maneuver in the Global Commons (JAM-GC), 3, 16, 21, 25
Joint Operational Access Concept (JOAC), 19, 20
Joint Publication (JP) 3–12, Cyberspace Operations (Department of Defense), 20

Kahn, Herman, 55
Korea. *See* North Korea; South Korea
Krepinevich, Andrew, 17, 18
Kugler, Richard, 59
Kwangmyong (North Korea), 68

L Root Server, 43
land A2/AD operations, 2, 14, *See also* A2/AD operations in other domains
land cables. *See* terrestrial cables
landing sites, cable, 5, 30–31

law enforcement, 29, 53
legal considerations, 23–24
Libicki, Martin, 57, 58
Libya, no-fly zones used against, 15
links, in BGP system, 45
Lipson, Howard, 57
logic layer of cyberspace, 5, 40–52
 function of, 6, 40
 protecting, 6, 7
 safeguards to protect, 40
 strategic attack on Internet and, 7
 types of threats and cyber attacks on, 6, 7, 40
 vulnerabilities of, 40
London Internet Exchange (LINX), 51
Lynn, William J. III, 2

Mahan, Sir Alfred T., 13, 74
Maloof, F. Michael, 37
Maness, Ryan C., 53
man-in-the-middle attacks, 46
maritime A2/AD operations, 2, 13, *See also* A2/AD operations in other domains
 advantages of, 13
 naval blockades in, 3, 13, 23, 24
Mazanac, Brian, 59
McConnell, Mike, 64
mechanical cyber attacks, 7
Meeting the Anti-Access and Area Denial Challenge (Krepinevich, Watts, and Work), 17
microsatellites, 32, 68
Middle East, military basing structure in, 80
militarization of cyberspace, 2
military bases, 68, 80
military conflicts
 coercion as option to, 54
 cyberspace as enabler of, 54
 strategic cyber A2/AD operation as part of, 53
 strategy of conflict and, 54
 threat of pain in, 55
mobile phones, 34
Moore's law, 32
Morgan, Patrick, 59
Moscow, Napoleon's march toward, 14

Napoleon, 14
*Nation Forsaken, A* (Maloof), 37
national policy, cyber deterrence theory and, 59
national security
 A2/AD in cyberspace as concern for, 19
 A2/AD operations in cyberspace and, 4
 Department of Defense on importance of cyberspace to, 4

EMP attacks and, 36
  projecting power globally for, 12
National Security Agency, EINSTEIN program of,
  79, 82
NATO, 71
natural disasters, 29, 30, 33
naval blockages
  anti-access operations using, 3, 13, 23, 24
  goal of, 13
navigation. freedom of, 12
Navy
  Air Sea Battle (ASB) concept of, 18
  directed energy weapons of, 36
  maritime A2/AD operations with, 13
Netnod, 43
network intrusions, 7, 66
network management systems, 6
network security firms, 50, 51
new triad, 66
New York City
  denial of service attack on ISP in, 48
  terrestrial cable networks near, 30
  trans-Atlantic cables near, 6, 27
no-fly zones
  anti-access as part of, 15
  area denial as part of, 3, 15
  destruction of land-based sensors and weaponry
    using, 15
  examples of reasons for imposing, 15
  military use of, 15
  ultimate goal of, 15
non-state actors, 16, 20, 56, 70, 80
  tailored deterrence against, 65
norm theory, 71
norms, in deterrence by cooperation, 62
North Atlantic Treaty Organization (NATO), 71
North Korea
  cyber attack (2014) on, 1, 68
  cyber force offensive capabilities of, 69
  denial of access as punitive sanction against, 77
  deterrence by denial approach to, 62
  global Internet connection infrastructure of, 62, 68
nuclear deterrence
  assumption of rationality in, 54
  cyberspace deterrence and applicability of, 57,
    58, 72
  differences between cyber and nuclear
    capabilities and, 57
  inherent sense of risk and, 55
  lessons for cyber deterrence from, 54–57
  leveraging for strategic A2/AD operations, 75
  new triad for, 57, 66
  post–Cold War challenges to, 56

punishment and denial as, 57
  robust defense in, 55
  strategic A2/AD operations compared with, 67
  strategies and capabilities updated for, 54
  strategy of conflict in, 54
  tailored deterrence in, 65
  threat of pain to civilian populations in, 55, 63
nuclear explosions
  EMP attacks using, 37, 38
  strategic A2/AD with, 67
nuclear facilities, as off-limits for cyber
    attacks, 82
nuclear warfare
  assumption of rationality in avoiding, 54
  Basic Principles Agreement rules on, 56
  possibility of, 54
  strategy of conflict against, 54
nuclear weapons
  cyber capabilities versus capabilities of, 57
  electromagnetic pulse from, 37, 38
  norm theory on use of, 71
  number of countries with, 56, 65
  outer space detonation of, 67
  Partial Test Ban Treaty (1963) on, 67
Nye, Joseph, 58, 59

O3b, 31
ocean A2/AD operations. *See* maritime A2/AD
    operations
oceans
  as buffer zones, 12
  fiber optic cables under, 5, 26
  submarine cables under, 26
oil industry, 13, 29
*One Second After* (Forstchen), 37
OODA loop theory, 4
open resolvers, in denial of service, 50
operating systems
  fiber optic cable vulnerabilities with, 6
  human interactions and vulnerability of, 7
operations in anti-access and area denial strategy.
    *See* A2/AD operations

Pakistan Telecom, 46
Pakistan, government blocking of YouTube in, 46
Paris terrorist attacks (2015), 22
Partial Test Ban Treaty (1963), 67
*PC World*, 50
peering among ISPs, 48
peers, in BGP system, 45
Persian Gulf, 13
physical layer of cyberspace, 5, 26–39
  elements of, 5, 26

physical layer of cyberspace (cont.)
    protecting, 7
    strategic attack on Internet and, 7
    types of attacks in, 5, 7
    vulnerabilities in, 5
political access denial, 18
political events, impact on A2/AD strategy of, 15
population centers. *See* civilian populations
power projection, 13, 20, 80
punishment, in deterrence, 60, 62

Quadrennial Defense Review (QDR),
    Department of Defense, 56, 57

radar, 34, 35
radio, 34
rationality assumption, in nuclear weapons use, 54
reconnaissance satellites, 68
redundancies
    ability to withstand major cyber attacks and, 8
    domain name systems (DNS) with, 6
Rensys, 46, 47
research questions, 9, 76
Rid, Thomas, 53
rights of way, for cables, 30
rogue states, 8, 16, 36, 65, 77, 80
root name servers, 43
root servers, 41–44
    attacks on, 43–44
    hostnames, IP addresss, and operators table
        for, 41
    number of, 41, 42
    recommendations for protecting, 44
    resiliency of, 43
    responsibilities of operators of, 42
    vulnerabilities of and safeguards with, 6, 40
root zones, 41
Russia
    Napoleon's march toward Moscow in, 14
    tailored deterrence against, 65

sanctuaries, 18
satellites, 31–33
    antisatellite missiles against, 32, 67
    challenes in using, 32
    ground stations with, 29, 33, 61
    hacking into, 33
    hardware capability and, 32
    imaging, 4, 68
    Iranian, 68
    microsatellites, 68
    physical layer of cyberspace with, 5
    reconnaissance, 68
    space debris as threat to, 32, 33

spy, 33
    submarine cable operations compared with, 31
    vulnerabilities of, 32, 33
    weather, 33
SCADA, 6, 64
Schelling, Thomas C., 54, 55, 62, 63, 64, 66
sea A2/AD operations. *See* maritime A2/AD
    operations
sea control, 13
sea lines of communication (SLOCs), 13
seas
    fiber optic cables under, 5, 26
    submarine cables under, 26
Security and Stability Advisory Committee
    (SSAC), 44
security firms, 50, 51
security forces, government, 53
server farms, 5, 26, 75, 81
servers
    human interactions and vulnerability of, 7
    physical layer of cyberspace with, 5, 26
    vulnerabilities of and safeguards with, 6, 40
session hacking, 45
Singer, Peter, 66
Smoke, Richard, 56
Snyder, Glynn, 55
Sony Pictures, cyber attack (2014) on, 1, 69, 79
South Korea, cyber attacks on financial institutions
    in, 69
Southwest Asia, conflicts in, 21
Soviet Union
    assumption of rationality in avoiding nuclear
        weapons use by, 54
    Partial Test Ban Treaty (1963) and, 68
    rules for détente with, 56
    tailored deterrence and, 56
space debris, and satellites, 32, 33
Space Systems/Loral, 31
space, primary mission of US armed forces in, 20
Spamhaus, 51
Spanish-American War, 27
speakers, in BGP system, 45
spoofing, 34, 44, 47, 50
spy satellites, 33
Strait of Hormuz, 13, 68
strategic A2/AD attacks
    escalation of military engagement as reaction
        to, 53
    impact on society of, 53
    Internet as focus of, 7
strategic cooperation, in cyber deterrence, 60
strategy in anti-access and area denial operations.
    *See* A2/AD strategy
strategy of conflict, 54

*Strategy of Conflict, The* (Schelling), 54
Stuxnet, 6
submarine cables, 26–29
  damage to, 27
  early use of, 27
  landing stations for, 30
  map of location, routes, and endpoints of, 27
  responsibility for avoiding, 29
  satellites compared with, 31
  telecommunications systems use of, 26
  types of, 27
Sun Tzu, 11
supervisory control and data acquisition system
  (SCADA), 6, 64
surveillance operations, 23, 67
Sustaining U.S. Global Leadership Priorities for
  21st Century Defense (Department of
  Defense), 20
system intrusions, 7, 66

tactical cooperation, in cyber deterrence, 60
tactical cyber A2/AD operations
  A2/AD strategy contrasted with, 4
  blocking access to specific portions of
    cyberspace in, 22
  description of, 4
  neutralizing a particular type of cyber attack
    in, 22
tailored deterrence, 65
  arguments for using, 59
  cyber proxies use and, 65
  description of, 56
  logic behind, 56
  number and type of actors in cyberspace
    complicating, 65
*Tallinn Manual on the International Law Applicable
  to Cyber Warfare. The* (Schmitt), 23, 71
Tangredi, Sam, 17
telecommunications
  cable landing site equipment for, 30
  early use of cables for, 27
  maps marking cables for, 29
  natural disasters damaging, 29
  satellite transmission in, 31
  submarine cables for, 26, 27
  vulnerabilities of, 37
telegraph cables, 27
telephone systems, 1, 48
terrestrial cables, 30–31
  damage to, 30
  parts of, 30
  physical protection for, 31
  vulnerabilities of, 30, 31

terrorist attacks, 22
terrorist networks, 36, 56, 65
third wave of deterrence theory, 56
Thomas, Timothy, 57
threat of pain
  coercion used with, 69
  deterrence using, 62
  deterrent to escalation using, 55
  nuclear deterrence and, 63
  strategic A2/AD operations and, 63
Tier 1 ISPs, 48
Tolou (Iranian reconnaissance satellite), 68
Transmission Control Protocol (TCP), 45, 49
treaties, possible A2/AD strategy conflicts with, 23
Tunisia, government monitoring of Internet in, 70

United Kingdom, Partial Test Ban Treaty (1963)
  and, 68
United Nations Committee on the Peaceful Uses
  of Outer Space, 68
United Nations Convention on the Law of the
  Sea, 12
United Nations Security Council, 23
United States
  A2/AD policy of, 16
  assumption of rationality in avoiding nuclear
    weapons use by, 54
  Cyberspace National Action Plan of, 21
  Partial Test Ban Treaty (1963) and, 68
  rules for détente and, 56
  vulnerability of, due to technological
    development, 64
  weather satellites of, 33
User Datagram Protocol (UDP), 49
user layer of cyberspace, 5, 6

Valeriano, Brandon, 53
Verisign, 42
ViaSat, 31
virus protection, 51
viruses, computer, 30, 51
volumetric attacks, in denial of service, 49
vulnerability
  four layers in cyberspace global grid and, 5
  human interactions and, 7
  planning and policy implications of, 7
  proliferation of and dependence on cyberspace
    and, 4
  strategic A2/AD attack on cyberspace and, 7
  US technological development resulting in, 64

Watts, Barry, 17, 18
weather satellites, 33

weather, as part of anti-access or area denial strategy, 14
web addresses, 41
Wheatley, Gary, 57
Windows operating system, 6
wireless Internet, 34, 48
Work, Robert O., 17, 18
worms, computer, 6, 30, 51

Wrenn, Christopher F., 60

Xerxes, 11, 13, 14

YouTube, 46

Zafar (Iranian imaging satellite), 68
zombie computers, 49, 51

Printed in the United States
by Baker & Taylor Publisher Services